# REVELATION
# AND EXPERIENCE

Edited by
## Edward Schillebeeckx
and
## Bas van Iersel

A CROSSROAD BOOK
The Seabury Press · New York

1979
The Seabury Press
815 Second Avenue
New York, N.Y. 10017

Library of Congress Catalog Card Number: 78-66133
ISBN: 0-8164-0392-9
ISBN: 0-8164-2609-0 (pbk.)
Printed in the United States of America

# CONTENTS

# Part III
## Revelation and Experience in Regard to Language and Society

# Part IV
## The Theology of Revelation Related to Experience

# Editorial

CRITICALLY subversive key-words have a tendency these days soon to degenerate to the level of fashionable words. This has certainly happened to the word 'experience'. At one time it was much maligned; for many years it was used critically and productively; and now it is already employed in a restorative sense. An appeal can be made to experiences both on the basis of critically subversive intentions and on the basis of restorative intentions. This is really quite important when it is remembered that experience has everything to do with revelation. By this we mean revelation in the universally human sense of 'I was suddenly struck by something', meaning 'it was a revelation to me'. We also mean revelation in the specifically Christian sense of the self-revelation of God in the man Jesus, in which we experience Christ as the salvation of all men.

Experience is a complex reality and, with revelation in mind, it must be considered as carefully as possible. The concept of experience has also to be examined. This will help to prevent misunderstandings in the use of a word which can point to completely different realities and emotions.

In the Old and New Testaments and in the period immediately following, what we now generally call 'experience' played an intermediary part of decisive importance. In the fifth century, however, at the end of classical and late classical antiquity, when the barbarian invasions brought chaos into the ancient world, the Christian Church was the only stable social factor. It was at this time that these new experiences began to lose their strength (with the accompanying loss of criticism of certain institutions). In the long run, experience even became suspect and the only valid factor was the authority of the 'book' (the record of a past civilization) and especially the book that the Church controlled—the Bible. There were repeated counter-movements, but any appeal made to experience was held in suspicion and played off against the practice of appealing to the Bible, the tradition and the teaching authority of the Church.

When the importance of critical reason was discovered during the Enlightenment, the problem of the normative power of experience became acute. The conviction that all truth was only to be found in the past was shattered and replaced by a faith in the intermediary part played by contemporary experience in the finding of new truth. The emergence of the experiential sciences gave rise to attempts to throw a rational light on our experiences.

It is demonstrable that, in the course of history, an appeal to experience has often been made at times when men have felt oppressed by others and especially by institutions. Men's awe and suspicion when confronted by new experiences (including mystical experiences) are nourished by two factors. On the one hand, there is a misleading identification, lacking in light and shade, of revelation either with a written book or with a purely conceptual deposit of faith and, on the other, a tendency to narrow the hermeneutical subject of the tradition of revelation down to the teaching authority of the Church. It has become clear that an appeal made to what is called 'immediate' experience is exposed to all kinds of impasses, especially if the genesis, the social and historical context, and the subconscious mediation of these experiences are not analyzed at the same time.

Christian theologians cannot be exclusively concerned with an analysis of conceptual expressions of earlier experiences. They have also to analyze new experiences and to try to find the earlier experiences that lie concealed behind earlier interpretations that seem to us to be superseded. In this way, they can perhaps discover the extent to which the identity of the Christian message or evangelical orientation is made present in such new experiences, or to which that message is alienated from itself. Contemporary experiences have a hermeneutical significance with regard to the content of Christian experience and knowledge: that is, they help us to understand that content. On the other hand, this specifically Christian experience and our reflection about it also have an original, critical and productive power to disclose our universally human experiences in the world.

The structure of this *Concilium,* which is devoted to dogma, can be seen from this brief outline of the problem. The number begins with an article in which the problem, in the form in which it appears again and again in Church circles, is situated and analyzed. The problem is that of the contrast between an appeal made to authority and an appeal made to experience. In this situation, many Christians experience an alienation between the institutions of the Church and their own historical world of experience (Peter Eicher). This problem calls for a more precise definition of what is meant by the complex reality that we call 'experience', a definition that should take two forms—a historical and a systematic definition. On the one hand, then, it is clear that, during the Enlightenment (and in this context we mean especially the German Enlightenment), reason became conscious of its critical and constructive possibilities in the experience of non-reason or non-sense in history and tried to illuminate experience with reason (Werner Schneiders). On the other hand, it can be demonstrated on the basis of the writings of two representatives of Catholic modernism, Alfred Loisy and George Tyrrell, that there was no single, unequivocal view in the Modernist movement about the part played by experience in the history of revelation (Jan Hulshof). The problem of what experience really is and of its meaning for revelation, which was not solved during the Enlightenment or the Modernist period and has not been solved since, calls for a systematic analysis of the whole complex concept of experience (Dietmar Mieth).

Christian revelation, which comes to us through human experience, is also for this reason connected with the question of language and the growing specification of experiences of revelation in a suitable language of faith (Robert Schreiter). This linguistic problem should not, however, be thought of as exclusively linguistic. There can be no experience of revelation without socio-historical mediation and revelation itself also has an intermediary part to play in the self-understanding of societies, if it is to have an ideological function. This question has been analyzed in this *Concilium* in two ways—historically and critically (Bernard Plongeron) and thematically (Matthew Lamb). In both cases, experience of revelation seems to imply a 'political theology', either in an affirmative (and restorative) direction or in a direction which opens the way to the future.

These articles have been included to prevent theological reflections from being understood in an idealistic way. They are followed by three specifically theological essays. In the first of these articles, the communal character of experiences of faith is discussed. The living community of faith, the Church as a whole, is seen as the subject of the interpretative experience of Christian faith (Carlo Molari). In the second, the fundamental question that is asked is to what extent can a particular tradition of experience, in this case the Jewish-Christian tradition, be the unique, decisive and total mediation of the Absolute. In other words, to what degree does the Christian revelation, in its historical particularity, coincide with the spiritual experience of the whole of mankind? (David Tracy). The third theological article deals with revelation and experience in connection with theology and spirituality (Heinrich Stirnimann).

The results of the articles in this *Concilium* may perhaps be used as a point of departure for a theory of tradition in which the part played by experience in the development of tradition can be indicated. They may also form an approach to a critical examination of experience and a questioning of the normative value of particular experiences in socio-historical conditions.

*Edward Schillebeeckx*
*Bas van Iersel*

# PART I

*The State of the Question*

Peter Eicher

# Administered Revelation: The Official Church and Experience

IF I DESCRIBE the relation between the official Church and experience as *alienated,* I imply not only a criticism of conditions within the Church but a problematic relation of the ecclesial institution to the historical world of experience. The reference-point for such a critique of alienation is, however, to be found in another, notionally possible condition of trust, solidarity and fruitful tension between the institutional Church and the contemporary experiential world, whether this condition is taken as positive and existing, or as possible in a future order of Christian communities. The following account is guided by the supposition that the development of ecclesial offices need not *eo ipso* lead to the alienation of the church leadership from experience, even though in the historical circumstances, alienation has become constitutive of such a relationship. Only, however, where the contradictions between an increasingly bureaucratized official Church and a world of experience isolated from it can be observed as inclusively as possible, can critical analysis itself help to destroy that alienation.

The following analysis is therefore directed first to the original question of the main aspects of ecclesiastical institutionalization, in order then to elicit the main theological problems of the new self-understanding of ecclesial office at Vatican I. This question has to be seen in terms of the historical development of modern society, if it is to be clearly understood in its full ambivalence in regard to the contemporary world. Conclusions are drawn in respect to those perspectives which became possible in the light of Vatican II, and which possibly point to a new relationship between the official Church and human experience.

3

## ALIENATION AS A RESULT OF THE INSTITUTIONALIZATION
## OF THE GOSPEL

The dissociation of the so-called official Church from particular instances of contemporary experience of reality has as many dimensions as an institutionalized church leadership has functions.[1] Hence, when one first considers these inner and outer functions of ecclesial office from the origins to the present, the extent of the tragic dilemma which apparently leads necessarily to the divergence of experience from institutionalization is clear. The external tensions of the institutional Church and historical experience correspond to the inner contradictions in the development of Christian church offices and the lived experience of faith in following Jesus.

### The institutional split

The essential aspects of the inner split arose from the need to take the original experience of faith from the eschatological situation of Jesus' disciples and retain it in historical time. The continuation provided by the 'official Church' eventually consisted of the Gospel and doctrine, the experience of salvation and administration of the sacraments, charismatic interaction and a hierarchical constitution of parishes or communities, an ethic of freedom and the moral law, and finally the biographical drama of individual conversion to religious formation.

In the situation of Jesus' kerygma the proclaimed kingdom of God was revealed as the initially apparent presence of the Lord to come. Jesus' parabolic discourse made this kingdom-to-come present in terms of everyday language and thus in everyday experience.[2] His miracles made the kingdom of God symbolically real and therefore capable of being experienced by those who heard his message. Jesus became, in his life, death and resurrection, an historical reality for his community, and one proclaimed and believed as the experiential, eschatological proximity of God. Even though this experience of the eschatological proximity of God is not to be misunderstood as a direct experience of God (it is, like all experience, mediated through tradition, language and symbolism) nevertheless the early prophetic proclamation of the Christian community shows that this experience was an original encounter in 'the Spirit', and therefore an elementary revelation encounter—and one so elementary that it cannot be represented as anything other than a 'vision' of the risen Lord.[3]

But the pastoral epistles already show the disappearance of that prophetic enactment and its replacement by committed doctrine,[4] which is to be preserved until Christ comes again (1 Tim 6:20; 2 Tim 1:14). Since the community produced general criteria for the discernment of sound doctrine and false gnosis (Tit 2), it also produced the religious specialists or morally qualified teachers who became responsible for handing on the original message and suppressing spontaneous prophecy. This beginning of the formation of ecclesial office shows that the preservation of the original experience of faith led to the institutionalized separation of teaching status and believing community, but also to the repression of prophetic gifts and the individual's charismatic experience of faith. The experience of the Gospel is mediated through adherence to church doctrine.

Jesus' joyous cry over Zacchaeus: 'Today salvation has come to this house!' (Lk 19:9) stands as a summary of what the eschatological prophet brought to those of his countrymen who did not reject the proclamation of the kingdom of God: the experiential *shalom* of the imminent last time, the revelation of the present as a time of judgment, the new justification of those excluded from salvation: in short, the experience of grace and judgment in an actual real-life situation. As, however, the Lukan addition to the synoptic account of the Last Supper shows ('Do this in memory of me' [Lk 22:19]), the death of Jesus came after a ritual enactment of that experience. The gradual establishment of the sacraments was intended to overcome the separation of the historical community from that original experience of salvation. But this ritualized compensation contained an ambivalence peculiar to worship and its rules: it offered both an enactment and an alienating routine; it annihilated the time which separated from salvation, but it also reified the appropriation of divine proximity. The experience of salvation was mediated sacramentally and therefore became ambivalent in regard to experience.

Jesus' unconditional call for followers and his symbolic summons to the Twelve did not constitute an office inseparable from the person selected, and one that could be assumed by others.[5] His call was addressed to the person as a person; it constituted discipleship and not an official Church. But the handing on of doctrine and the administration of the sacraments throughout history led to firmly prescribed functions which devolved on those selected in accordance with specific criteria. The office and the holder of that office were differentiated.[6] But that also implied a separation in principle of the personal experience and specific quality of the officeholder from his prescribed function. Office was exercised in accordance with suprapersonal criteria. The rôle was decisive and not the unique experience of the officeholder. This distinction guaranteed the continuity of teaching and the mediation of salvation, but it condemned the salvation that had been mediated to an impersonal status and exclusion from the area of experience, and in extreme cases meant that the officeholder could be a functionary.

Jesus' message about the kingdom of God had unconditionally ethical consequences, because God's gesture made the conversion of existence possible; but the indicative of grace remained of primary importance; in other words the elementary experience of salvation which made a new *ethos* possible came first. But for the greater Church, the necessity arose of laying down criteria for membership of the community of believers in terms of general laws, which concerned not the experience of salvation but testable morality. But this codification again changed the appeal to historical existence into the imperative of conformity with a set of rules, which led in the best case to domination of the history of freedom by fixed norms, and in the worst to legalistic alienation from that very history of freedom.

Finally, the difference between Jesus' method of summoning disciples and the teaching methods of the rabbis[7] is shown in the fact that Jesus aimed at conversion and not at instruction; at the reversal of biography and not at the furtherance of theology. But the continuance of what the original community had learnt from Jesus became the formation of doctrinal formulae, catechisms and rules of faith, and finally the development of a special scholasticism.[8] With the introduction of infant baptism the drama of conversion fully entered the regulative field of education and public instruction with their tendency to general rôle formation.

The difference between individual experience and institutionalized religiosity is the price which Christianity paid for its own continuity. As O'Dea says, religion needs institutionalization, but suffers from it.[9] It needs office in order to resist chaos and collapse under a mass of individualisms; it needs the magisterium for simplification and insurance against dissolution into arbitrary theory; it needs the prescription of an ethics in order to produce precise behaviour patterns and rôles; it needs a court of appeal to co-ordinate and control, but all that contributes simultaneously to the loss of its creative power, and frustrates creative individualism, as well as weakening individual responsibility by too great a degree of stabilization. The Church tends then to bureaucratize salvation itself through its official administration, and alienates the faithful from their particular needs, and thus reifies religiousness. It replaces the living drama of faith with the recurrence of the same rôles.

## The external ambivalence of institutionalization

The ambivalence of the external functions of the official Church corresponds to this inward ambiguity. Hence the task of the missions requires constant translation from a particular situation of Christian faith into the universal concepts of a world Church. The non-situational nature of the official language of the Church is the fatal consequence of the necessity of speaking 'for everyone'. The inner universality of the message also demands external confrontation with particular power conditions and, by a sublime tactical adaptation, leads fatally to the development of power on the model of state and social partners. Since the ecclesial structures of domination are legitimized religiously, the official Church loses its flexibility and remains within permanently ar-chaic structures. Its official structure no longer corresponds to the way in which a particular age experiences authority; instead it reproduces that of the past. This non-contemporaneity of the forms of rule easily leads to a non-contemporaneity of ecclesial apologetics, which tries to reject as error anything that fits the experience of contemporaries but does not accord with the data of history. In this way the official Church threatens to become culturally non-contemporaneous and thus to alienate itself from contemporary experience as a whole.

## Not only a linguistic problem

The word 'experience' always refers to an actual situation; it needs the irreplaceable individual as a subject and always intends something new as against a preceding interpretation. 'Office', on the other hand, does not refer to situations by definition. It does not need a unique individual as a subject but an educated and adaptable mediator of the general rather than the particular. Offices do not of themselves bring something new into existence but dominate and administer what is continued from the past. The constitutive difference between the origi-nal situation of Christian proclamation and the need to make it ordinar-ily relevant by means of institutionalization shows the short-circuit operating when theologians and officeholders only ask one question: 'Why doesn't the grass-roots Catholic accept the Church's teaching any longer? How are we to speak if we want to understand people today.' The separation of office and experience shows that it is not really a language problem but one of the institutional existence of reli-gion as a whole. I shall now examine this problem, and ask whether the alienation of the authority of the magisterium from the authority of experience[10] is characteristic of modern Catholicism.

### EXPERIENCE OF REVELATION AND ECCLESIAL AUTHORITY

The dichotomy between the experience of faith and the magisterium appears in the Constitution on Faith of Vatican I. This Council set against the experience of autonomous rationalism and the self-determination of revolutionary practice the unconditional authority of the self-revealing God validly interpreted by the 'infallible' authority[11] of the magisterium. Though the modern era made scientifically demonstrable universal validity a criterion of legitimate experiential knowledge, and the quality of freedom the criterion of legitimate rule, Vatican I subjected these criteria for all valid experience to the authority of the magisterium. But the magisterium—and this is the decisive point—no longer, like Trent, ensured the certainty of pronouncements about faith by recourse to the truth of the Gospel, but by citing the authority of the revealing God.[12] Faith would then mean holding what God revealed 'to be true and doing so not on account of the intrinsic truth of things, which we recognize by the natural light of reason, but on account of the authority of the revealing God'.[13] Here there are at least two problems which concern on the one hand the relation between revelation and the experience of faith, and on the other the relation between the magisterium and experience as a whole.

## From revelation as event to revealed dogma

There is no doubt that as far as biblical and patristic tradition (still effective in the Tridentine understanding of faith[14]) were concerned, revelation was to be experienced and theologically reflected on in practical faith as a contemporary event.[15] The differentiation between revealed articles of faith, which are evident only to God, and the range of experience of what is revealed (*revelabile*) through the article of faith (a distinction made against the Arab Enlightenment) led for the first time in Aquinas[16] to that ultimately fatal separation which presented revelation no longer as something contemporaneous in faith but as something that was in principle closed off: an event henceforth to be explained by the magisterium alone. The anti-reformation theological criteriology of authentic belief (Cano, Bellarmine, Suarez, and so on) made the problem more acute, because universal rules were established to secure the consensus of faith as a criterion of truth. That meant that the sense of faith as an individual and collective organ of discernment of the event of revelation[17] was subordinated to a criteriology of rational-theological statement. Confession and conviction were subordinated to theologically articulated dogma and the testimony of Scripture became a mere proof of official doctrine. And the word of God threatened to sink below dogma.[18] This was very clear in the ever-stronger tendency against the modern Enlightenment which became apparent in apologetics, and which Vatican I elevated to magisterial status. Henceforth dogma no longer appeared as regulator of the ecclesial language of faith; but the theologically formulated dogma itself was revealed truth (*divinitus revelatum dogma*).[19] Finally revelation became doctrine. It no longer qualified the experience of faith but henceforth characterized its ultimate ground of legitimation.

## Supernatural legitimation as against modern experience

The notion of faith offered at Vatican I seems no less significant in regard to the relation of office and experience as a whole. Where the authority of the revealing of God has become a formal criterion of faith, this infallible divine authority also has to be mediated historically through an ecclesial magisterium. But, as Archbishop Gasser put it in the official formulation, that 'cannot be demonstrated other than through the teaching Church'.[20] This also means that the teaching Church enters an authoritarian cycle, and legitimates the infallible authority of God by means of its own infallible authority. Its authority remains an authority communicated by God but in such a way that, as Gasser puts it, 'it can be deduced from the revelation of the will of Christ'[21] and therefore can be 'revealed *eo ipso*'[22] for the believer, obtaining validity only by way of the infallible interpretative authority which the magisterium exercises with the assistance of the Holy Spirit.

When the self-foundation of the magisterium reaches this ultimate formal hierarchy and the Church pronounces itself revealed in its very structure, as it is, then the problem of authority and experience is posed once again in all its poignancy. The scientifically explained experience of modern times, the suffering experience of everyday life as illumined by literature, and the unarticulated life-experience of the nameless millions without any apparent relationship with God, is no longer testified to by the authority of lived experience of faith, but is ultimately confronted by the sterile claim of a quite non-experiential and formal authority. The confrontation no longer takes place on the same level; it is not the experience of faith but supernatural legitimation which is opposed to experience of the world. The struggle of the drama of salvation cannot break out, for it is already resolved, already decided by the authority of the magisterium as 'a kind of supercriterion' (Kasper),[23] which depends on a presumed harmony between scientific results, everyday experience and magisterial decision, and thereby escapes the dialectic of experience. In this way, not only is the scientifically articulated experience of the world emptied of its critical validity for religious experience, but the faith-experience of the laity is also bereft of its own function. The infallibility of the ecclesial sense of fact, indwelling in all Christians, becomes a dead reflection of what has been authoritatively stated to be safe to believe and therefore becomes a purely passive infallibility.

Here there is an obvious danger. Revelation threatens to become administered, and administered by an ecclesial administration which escaped from the experiential and libertarian history of this age in order to withdraw into the formal legitimacy of a supernaturally guaranteed authority. Before I come to those aspects which in the ever-widening circle of Vatican II have led to the collapse of that kind of administered salvation, I must give a more detailed description of the nature of an authoritatively controlled religion in its relation to modern society.

## THE AMBIGUITY OF ADMINISTERED RELIGION IN A HIGHLY-DIFFERENTIATED SOCIETY

A theologian might be tempted to confront the inner differentiation of ecclesial offices and their increasing self-legitimation directly with biblical patterns and theological ideas. Since in doing that he reduces the social conditioning of the development of those official structures to become the will of the bearers of power in the Church, he overlooks the power of the laws of social developmental processes and ends up by making a moral appeal to officeholders or to some utopian project.[24] The approach of the sociology of religion since Max Weber[25] shows on the other hand—especially today in its socio-philosophical form in the works of Thomas Luckmann[26] and in its system-theoretical evaluation in the works of Niklas Luhmann[27]—the internal congruence and difference of church structures and the experiential world in the development of modern society. These functional analyses offer a more highly-nuanced picture of the modern dichotomy between the official Church and the experiential world.

## The isolation of the societas perfecta from the differentiated society

The modern magisterial notion of revelation and the consequently conditioned separation from the structure of modern experience represents a reaction to the fragmentation and differentiation of society which were characteristic of the bourgeois world in the revolutionary transition from the feudal order. The primary differentiation of state and society led, as a result of industrialization and the associated separation of capital and labour, to a secondary differentiation of all social sub-systems, such as family, churches, educational establishments, and so on, within the overall coherence of the total society. The Churches not only ceased to be a corpus christianum structuring society as a whole, but now found themselves confronting a large number of relatively autonomous institutional areas which no longer legitimized themselves sacrally, but found their meaning in their own functional environment. But in this way the church institutions lost the social basis of their specific structure and their mode of instruction. The Church itself became an institution specializing in religion and thereby structurally isolated from the mutually relatively independent experiential and normative environments of social reality. As far as the relation between the official Church and experience is concerned, this means that religious standardization and doctrine can no longer in principle lay claim to the entire range of experience of the individual in society, but only to its religious sector.

In the highly-differentiated society, the Church had to choose. Either it continued to lay claim to the whole man in his whole area of experience, and thereby in principle to withdraw him from modern society, or it accepted the privatized and autonomous individual as a self-sufficient bearer of responsibility in self-sufficient areas of responsibility, and could accordingly henceforth understand itself as a bearer of a free challenge and message to a free citizen of the world. The Church of Vatican I chose with all its consequences to take up a position over against modern society and chose thereby isolation from the historical experience of the modern era. It did this, however (and this was decisive for modern Catholicism), not only by an infallible retention of traditional doctrine, but also by retaining an historically exhausted form of feudalism and sovereign absolutism. In contrast to a highly-differentiated modern world with its informal groups, organizational units, social formation and national states, the Catholic Church defined itself as a *societas perfecta,* as a spiritual Church-state, and its organizational structure as the *corpus Christi mysticum.*[28] Tight central control was intended to compensate for the loss of effective power and plausibility through changes in the social context. In a society which no longer behaved in the manner of the feudal or corporate state, but operated functionally, a hierarchical corporate constitution could only survive if organized with extreme severity—like an army on foreign soil.

## Exhaustion and isolation

The self-assertion of the Catholic Church stood out like some monstrous aberration from the extreme differentiation of modern society; the consequences of the phenomenon have to be grasped dialectically. On the one hand, there was an intensified apartness from the nature of the modern era, a complete lack of adaptation, and an experience of divine power in worship and dogma opposed to all temporal conditions; on the other hand, the religious individual immunized himself precisely with such means against any consistent penetration of all areas of experience with religious content, and *vice versa*. The stable behaviour of officeholders and of the faithful was paid for with an immense loss of experience, and also a reduced religious responsibility. A highly rationalized form of religious domination was accompanied by a religious practice which found consolation not in religious life but in obedience to the rules. The relation to tradition made possible by this kind of Catholicism had a similarly ambivalent effect: on the one hand the fixed mediation of doctrine made possible a fruitful combination of traditional and new experience; on the other, dogmatized tradition blocked the way to any creative future, because it was understood as a collection of doctrines and no longer as a living process, as the historical action of the Spirit. 'The past is our future': the closure of religious tradition to new experience cannot be expressed more poignantly than in this declaration of Archbishop Lefèbvre's.[29] Just as ambivalent is the relation of official church dogma to the historical experience of contemporary men. On the one hand we have what Robert Musil expressed so well: 'Principles, guidelines, models, limitations are power batteries'[30] which seem to force people towards historical experience; on the other hand precisely these dogmatic power sources, because they are positivistically set over against historical experience, can restrain and suppress that experience.

The presuppositions of a mediation of religion that is optimally efficient and rational from the viewpoint of technical administration have disappeared in modern society. It was almost the very rigidity and strictness of the Vatican I conception which rendered fragile, even if it did not destroy, this idea in Vatican II.

### RECONCILIATION OF REVELATION AND HISTORICAL EXPERIENCE

It would be a fundamental misunderstanding of the modern situation if we were to attribute all the guilt for the separation of religion and the experiential world to the official Church's conception of itself. The development of modern theology in the Protestant Churches, too, shows that this alienation was not merely a special problem for officeholders, but a result of the increasing scientization of all areas of life; of the technical reification and availability of nature; and of the 'total administration' of all aspects of life.[31] The official Catholic Church's fear of new experience is only a fragment of the total social alienation between institutionality and privatized experience, the mediation of tradition and formation of the future, myth and science, and religion and the technical world. This does not stop theological reflection, so long as it has not immunized itself against experience as a whole, helping to cancel that alienation.

## A new thrust in theology?

In accordance with the separation of the magisterium from the scientifically-articulated experience of life characteristic of the modern age, the mainstream of modern theology has protected itself with a kind of open or implicit positivism against the powerful flood of new experiences in psychological and sociological, historical and natural-scientific, epistemological and religious studies (to name only the most important areas). The result of this wariness of a theology that would include empirical experience in its scientifically-mediated form as a constitutive part of its reflection, is that: 'We can only believe in God in spite of experience' (Bultmann).[32]

The basis of this immunization from experience differs according to the theoretical and ecclesial standpoint of a particular theology, but usually derives from a positivism which is apparently beyond all criticism from the experiential world.[33] For Karl Barth, this positive element is to be found in the state of eternal election, which becomes history as supra-history in Jesus Christ, without being empirically pre-accessible. For Rudolf Bultmann, it is to be found in the eternal word of reconciliation which only paradoxically affects history, and which remains non-objectifiable and therefore absolutely closed to experience. Everything given and perceptible becomes an 'indication' without any specific religious substance, a symbol without any representational power, a sign without any significance. In a structurally similar way, in Jürgen Moltmann's theology of hope, history can only be conceived henceforth as the non-enactment of a salvation conceived in an apocalyptic future. In Catholic theology, the experiential world is in principle allowable as a possible *analogon* to divine reality, yet in the phenomenology of Hans Urs von Balthasar the experiential world of history is no less excluded than is the social, psychological and political world of lived experience from the transcendental theology of Karl Rahner.[34] By recourse to the strictly impenetrable transcendentality of unending mystery, this theology in its own way takes refuge from actual confrontation with all the areas of empirical experience.

It is the work of a hermeneutics which has come to see the biblical text once again as the expression of an historical experience of God, and revelation as living encounter with the actuality of the experiential world, to see this profound alienation as removable at least within a projected reconciliation of revelation and history. For Protestant theology, the work of Wolfhart Pannenberg does this in trying to grasp historical experience in the context of its traditional history. In Catholic theology the function is performed by Walter Kasper's theology. Kasper has tried to show that only by traversing the negation (Hegel) which reveals the untruth of knowledge hitherto, is it possible for experience to prevail against predetermined theories and faith-projects[35]: the 'unbearable discrepancy of faith and experience'[36] can be cured only if the continuity of tradition is ensured and vitally retained in that particular discontinuity. 'Therefore, in theology we are called not merely to think from the basis of the internal systematics of our dogmatic or biblical formulas and concepts, but much more from the basis of actual experiential reality'.[37]

## The compromise of Vatican II

At two decisive points the upheavals of the last conciliar debate took the relation between ecclesial doctrine and experiential reality to a new level: first, by a new relation between revelation and history, second by the notion of permanent church reform, and a new valuation of the prophetic experience of the laity.

In spite of the initial attempts of Roman scholastic theology to interpret the decree on revelation entirely as a purely magisterial administration of revelation, the Council experienced a theology of the word contributed by the Secretariat for Christian Unity, and a salvation-history notion of revelation: 'The economy of salvation is realized by deeds and words, which are intrinsically bound up with each other. As a result, the works performed by God in the history of salvation show forth and bear out the doctrine and realities signified by the words; the words, for their part, proclaim the works . . .' (*Dei Verbum*, 2). In answer to the question of what those works might be, and whether only miracles were referred to, the theological commission said: 'the "works" referred to in the text are not only miracles but all salvific events',[38] and that means 'God's action in an historically-conditioned setting, the entry of revelation into history itself' (G. Blum).[39] That not only leads to the interrogation of the text of Scripture (on the positive basis of historico-critical research) about what kind of history it is expressing, but to the fact that history (now no longer conceived in its 'particularity') may now be assigned the status of revelation. For theology and the magisterium that means, however, that they have to inquire yet again into the meaning of history, and consequently into historically experienced reality, in order to treat revelation appropriately on the basis of its actual location.

In view of the continuous emphasis at Vatican II on the hierarchical constitution of the people of God and the *essential* difference between clergy and laity (*Lumen gentium*, 10), it may seem excessive to speak of a permanent reform of the Church, and accordingly of a new openness to the present experiential world. But it certainly accords with the inclusion of modern pluralist experience in the teaching methodology of the Church that the Council, in addition to a very rigid retention of traditional concepts, stressed the fact that the Church acknowledges—precisely because it is a holy Church—that it is always in need of purification. It 'continually takes the way of penance and renewal' (*Lumen gentium*, 8). This *renovatio continua* has also led to the beginnings of a new view of the inclusion of lay experience in ecclesial faith, in so far as (and here the Council astonishingly calls on the Reformed notion of office) the experience of the laity shares in the priestly, prophetic and royal offices of Christ (*De apostolatu laicorum*, 9-14). Yet this participation remains to all intents and purpose wholly passive, as far as its admission by the Church in terms of ordination and jurisdiction is concerned. But the layman is made all the more responsible for concern for secular areas; he has to approach them with the leaven of Christian life'. But here again there is a dilemma, because then the official Church again indirectly escapes responsibility for the world, and any practical concern with the contemporary experiential world; and leaves it to the laity, to the mere laity of this 'world', who are not allowed to contribute their faithful experience and competence to the doctrinal work of the Church.

The compromise apparent in the conciliar texts therefore leads no less effectively than the new emphasis in theology to a new consideration of the relation between the official Church and experience. It is possible that the historically effective nature of the revelation history testified to by Christians, here too, will produce something entirely new: something that is already beginning to break through, even though we are hardly as yet aware of it.

*Translated by V. Green*

## Notes

1. There are as yet no sociological micro-analyses of the behaviour of holders of church offices in regard to the world of contemporary experience. On the fundamental problems of the sociological analysis of religious experience, and the problem of the ecclesial institutionalization of the experience of faith in general, see (as introductory treatments): F. Fürstenberg (ed.), *Religionssoziologie* (second ed., Neuwied-Berlin, 1970); F. Haarsma, W. Kasper & F. X. Kaufmann, *Kirchliche Lehre* (Freiburg im Breisgau, 1970), cited as Haarsma; J. Wössner, *Religion im Umbruch* (Stuttgart, 1972); F. X. Kaufmann, *Theologie in soziologischer Sicht* (Freiburg im Breisgau, 1973); G. Milanesi, *Sociologia della Religione* (Turin, 1973); idem., *Religionssoziologie* (Zürich, 1976).

2. Cf. P. Eicher, *Solidarischer Glaube* (Düsseldorf, 1975), pp. 39-49; idem, 'Gott-Sagen', in *Kat. Blätter,* 101 (1976), pp. 717-31.

3. Cf. especially, R. Pesch, *Jesu ureigene Taten* (Freiburg im Breisgau, 1970).

4. Cf. G. Lohfink, 'Die Normativität der Amtvorstellungen in den Pastoralbriefen', in *ThQ,* 157 (1977), pp. 93-106.

5. Cf. M. Hengel, *Nachfolge und Charisma* (Berlin, 1968), pp. 68 ff.

6. Cf. J. Neumann, 'Die wesenhafte Einheit von Ordination und Amt', in F. Klostermann, ed., *Der Priestermangel und seine Konsequenzen* (Düsseldorf, 1977), pp. 95-128.

7. Hengel, op. cit., pp. 46-93.

8. Cf. W. Jaeger, *Das frühe Christentum und die griechische Bildung* (Berlin, 1963); Eng. trans., *Early Christianity and Greek Paideia* (Cambridge, Mass., 1961).

9. T. F. O'Dea, 'Five Dilemmas in the Institutionalization of Religion', in *Social Compass,* 7 (1960), pp. 61-67, 62.

10. Cf. E. Schillebeeckx, *Christus und die Christen* (Frieburg im Breisgau, 1977), pp. 20-56.

11. Archbishop Gasser in the official exposition of *Dei Filius,* Mansi 52, 1204B.

12. Cf. P. Eicher, *Offenbarung-Prinzip neuzeitlicher Theologie* (Munich, 1977), I.

13. DS 3008.

14. Cf. J. Ratzinger, 'Ein Versuch zur Frage des Traditionsbegriffs', in K. Rahner & J. Ratzinger, *Offenbarung und Überlieferung* (Freiburg im Breaigau, 1965), pp. 25-69.

15. Cf. Eicher, *Offenbarung,* op. cit., introduction.

16. Cf. especially, E. Gilson, *Le Thomisme* (Paris, sixth ed., 1965), pp. 16ff.

17. Cf. M. Seckler, 'Glaubenssinn', in *LThK* IV (Freiburg im Breisgan, second ed., 1960), cols., 945-48.

18. Cf. W. Kasper, *Dogma unter dem Wort Gottes* (Mainz, 1965).

19. DS, 3073.

20. Mansi, 1207A.

21. Mansi, 1214B.

22. Mansi, 1226A.

23. W. Kasper, 'Zum Problem der Rechtgläubigkeit in der Kirche von Morgen', in Haarsma, op. cit., pp. 37-96, 50.

24. Cf., without any attention to the sociological and canon law debate, G. Hasenhüttl, *Charisma, Ordnungsprinzip der Kirche* (Freiburg im Breisgau, 1969).

25. On recent discussion, cf. C. Seyfarth & W. Sprindel, eds., *Seminar: Religion und gesellschaftliche Entwicklung* (Frankfurt, 1973).

26. Cf. especially T. Luckmann, *Das Problem der Religion in der modernen Gesellschaft* (Freiburg im Breisgau, 1963), esp. pp. 53-77.

27. N. Luhmann, *Funktion der Religion* (Frankfurt, 1977).

28. Cf. K. Walf, 'Die katholische Kirche: eine "societas perfecta"', in *ThQ,* 157 (1977), pp. 107-18.

29. Quoted in *Frankfurter Rundschau,* 30.6.77, no. 148, p. 3.

30. R. Musil, *Der deutsche Mensch als Symbol* (Hamburg, 1967), p. 33.

31. Cf. especially H. Marcuse, *One-dimensional Man* (Boston & London, 1965).

32. R. Bultmann, *Jesus Christus und die Mythologie* (Hamburg, 1964), p. 99.

33. For a detailed exposition, see Eicher, *Offenbarung,* op. cit., and for a summary treatment, idem, 'Das Offenbarungsdenken in seiner katechetischen Konsequenz', in *Kat. Blätter,* 101 (1976), pp. 289-305.

34. See Eicher, *Die anthropologische Wende* (Freiburg im Uechtland, 1970).

35. Cf. Kasper, in Haarsma, op. cit., pp. 89-96; cf. Schillebeeckx, op. cit.

36. W. Kasper, *Glaube und Geschichte* (Mainz, 1970), p. 127.

37. Ibid., p. 143.

38. Unpublished thesis, p. 5.

39. G. Blum, *Offenbarung und Überlieferung* (Göttingen, 1971), p. 30.

# PART II

*In Search of a Definition of Experience*

Werner Schneiders

# Experience in the Age of Reason

## THE DISCOVERY OF REASON AND EXPERIENCE

THE AGE of the Enlightenment is usually known as the age of reason. This description, which derives from the self-observation of an intellectual tendency which was dominant for most of the eighteenth century and was found primarily in Scotland, France, Germany and England, is certainly not without justification. Reason was of course a key word of the Enlightenment, though the terms 'reason' (*ratio*) and 'understanding' (*intellectus*) varied in acceptation and in relation to one another. Reason was generally taken as a capacity for increasing insight into truth and untruth, but also as a norm for thought and action. Reason was not taken as autonomous purely and simply, but as a formally or substantially independent organ of control.

The initially ever-stronger tendency of the Enlightenment to appeal to reason can be explained only by a new experience of reason which began in the Middle Ages. After the first successes of theoretical reason in the modern sciences, and the philosophical self-assurance of reason in the self-constitution of reflection and methodology (for instance with the end of the Thirty Years' War), there was a general tendency to recourse to an auto-normative authority. In that view, reason is not ultimately conscious of the possibility of experiencing the un-reason of reality. Instead it sees itself in a critical and constructive capacity. Then there was an increasing reversal of rational construction in empirical criticism, based on new experience in politics and religion from the end of the seventeenth century. This was the beginning of the actual age of Enlightenment in the sense of the epoch of criticism.

With the revaluation of reason, there came a revaluation of experience as the basis of thought and action; this had occurred in principle since the Middle Ages, and happened at first without any essential conflict between reason and experience as two instances of appeal.

21

This re-estimation of reason and experience as normative forces was, of course, no accident. Ultimately, it derived from the fact that tradition (both of belief and of knowledge) was no longer adequately supportive. With the disappearance of the confidence that all truth had already been discovered or revealed in the past and remained only to be rediscovered, hope settled now on the truth of the present and of the future, and thus of research. Experience as direct encounter with present reality, or as an experimentally planned and controlled discovery of reality, would be the basis of thought and action. With the disappearance of religious belief, confidence—or at least hope—in reason and experience as supportive instances increased. Experience, like reason, was so to speak discovered anew; and both, in their relation to one another too, underwent a change in significance.

Reason, one might say in short, could become independent of the dominance of a supra-rational faith only by recourse to rationally trustworthy experience. It experienced itself largely as the rational extension of experience by means of the control and processing of sense experience. Therefore it tried to ground itself in experience without making itself dependent on experience. It even attempted to make experience as it were rational, by making *planned* experiences. Experience nevertheless remained a subordinate instance; and with the increased self-awareness of reason was even neglected and repressed. On the other hand, with the success of the new experiential sciences, there was greater insight into the necessity of experience. Therefore an explanation of what experience is and affords was all the more urgent. Hence, against the background of the common prospects and concurrence of reason and experience, even as early as the seventeenth century, there was an extension of modern cognition theory. Reason tried to understand experience and itself in regard to experience.

In view of the subsequent multiple views of experience, and reason and experience, in the eighteenth century, the widespread equation of the Enlightenment with rationalism is misleading, in other respects than epistemology. It is countered by the no less widespread idea that in Britain at least empiricism ruled almost unassailed, and with the beginning of the Enlightenment spread to France and Germany. But this idea, in spite of its accuracy in certain respects, is still lacking in understanding of the subtleties of the case, for there has never been a pure rationalism or a pure empiricism. Since, however, a critical account of the history of the modern theory of knowledge is impossible here, the following remarks are put forward only as an exemplary survey of a few known aspects of the German Enlightenment. As far as possible, I shall include certain aspects of the problem of experience in the eighteenth century which have not been treated by epistemologists.

## THE DEBATE ABOUT REASON AND EXPERIENCE

The interpretation of experience was governed right into the eighteenth century by notions developed by Aristotle and passed on by the Scholastics. For Aristotle experience was not set over against reason but, as a kind of practical knowledge in the field of particulars, formed a preliminary stage of rational knowledge on the basis of general principles. Yet in experience seen as the actualization of many particulars, the general might also be revealed, without any need for a supra-sensory perception of ideas or essences in the Platonic sense. This empiricism was subsequently constantly modified, and especially as far as the divisions of knowledge were concerned, but remained almost self-evident in epistemology, even when the practice of cognition in physics and metaphysics was often very distant from that notion.

Its first *de facto* fundamental extension to modern empiricism occurred at the beginning of the modern period with the general recognition of the necessity of experimentation: that is, of methodical planning. This happened not so much with Bacon, who intended to abstract knowledge systematically from a number of planned experiments, as with Galileo, who reduced individual experience defined by experimentation to its function of verification or falsification of a mathematical theory. Yet the epistemological significance of experimentation, and its consequences as far as the conceptualization of experience was concerned, was not recognized for a long time. Instead the function of experience and of experimentation in cognition was almost completely played down, even as early as Descartes. His own search for a firm ground for a new scientific philosophy was itself inspired by specific experiences, but Descartes, clinging to Platonic and Augustinian traditions, believed essentially that it was possible to obtain knowledge with the aid of certain innate ideas, especially the idea of God, and by means of rational analysis of the contents of consciousness. He also thought that this was possible on the basis of intuition (not conceived as experience) of the irrefragable existence of the ego or self-consciousness.

Only in the criticism of this position, which also appeared in another form in Britain, did modern Lockean empiricism make an appearance. It had already been conceived before 1670, but was made partially public only in 1688, and in 1690 in its full form. It became really known on the Continent only with the French translation of 1700. Locke (who himself had no special interest in the natural sciences) tried explicitly to derive all knowledge (apart from mathematics) from experience: that is, from mere sensual experience. He conducted his argument mainly in terms of epistemology. For him, experience was both the material of knowledge and the ultimate criterion of its truth. The inconsistencies and vaguenesses of his conception very soon led to the dissolution of this novel and, in intention at least, strict empiricism. On the one hand, it gave way to a form of subjective idealism which tried to keep to the so-called naked facts, and on the other hand to a complex of empirical and above all psychological and historical research which took effect, on the Continent too, from about the middle of the eighteenth century.

The development of epistemological debate in Germany, which took place for the most part only incidentally in the field of logic, was at first almost untouched by this process. Leibniz, of course, who held fundamentally to the notion of innate ideas, even extended this conception so that, from a divine viewpoint, everything was innate, even what from our viewpoint was a matter of experience. But Leibniz had already written an extensive treatise against Locke, although for quite different reasons it remained unpublished, and therefore ineffective, until 1765. In fact, at the beginning of the Enlightenment in Germany, both before and after the appearance of Locke's research, epistemology was still essentially dominated by a form of Aristotelian empiricism which in intention converged with Lockean empiricism, and therefore soon combined with it, though in actual execution it was still a long way behind it.

Christian Thomasius, though not a significant epistemologist, was in many respects exemplary of those who derived notions from experience in the early German Enlightenment. After his rejection in 1687 of the assumption of real innate ideas as scholastic, though he had acknowledged the existence of possible ideas that might be rendered actual through experience, Thomasius agreed in 1688 with the general conviction of the Aristotelians that there was nothing in the understanding that was not previously present in the senses; he concluded that sensory perception was the highest criterion of truth, without however expressly mentioning experience. In addition, he proceeded unthinkingly from experience in the sense of the practical certainty of the general, to experience in the sense of inductive experimentation. For him, as we can see from his 1691 *Introduction to the Theory of Reason,* experience was primarily the specific enactment of reality (by sensory perception), in contradistinction to mere book learning.

This corresponds to a scarcely examined and often hardly cited reference to experience which shows clearly how much Thomasius intended to ground, and did ground, his argument on so-called living experience. Hence he grounded his rejection of traditional opinions on the basis of wholly individual experiences: for example, the fact that he had learnt only through encountering Catholics how religiously prejudiced he in fact was. He was never reluctant to draw conclusions of

principle from private experiences of this kind, which in certain instances he found very hard to take. In addition, however, in his emphasis on the necessity of history (as the narrative account of past
events as a collection of facts or testimonies of alien experience), he
also made an attempt to make use of a knowledge of facts that extended
beyond his own circle of experience. In this sense, even religious
truths, wherever they did not correspond to independent rational
truths, were for the whole Enlightenment no more than historical
truths, even though the German Enlightenment did not draw anti-
Christian conclusions from this assumption.

The rise of the German Enlightenment was dominated by Christian
Wolff, who obeyed the scientific ideal proper to mathematics. He was a
thoroughly dogmatic rationalist who tried to derive all knowledge from
a few fundamental concepts. Wolff not only wrote an empirical
psychology and an experimental physics, but also stressed in his logic
the fact that original concepts and propositions were obtainable not by
means of explanation but initially only through experience. Even the
knowledge of the function of understanding relied on experience.
Therefore it is not astonishing that Wolff relied increasingly on experience, and was only hesitant in this regard because he feared that he
would be accused of subjectivity. He understood experience itself as
conscious sensual perception, leading to unique individual judgment
and to actualized ideas present in the aspect of possibility.

A new and stronger recourse to experience occurred only after the
middle of the eighteenth century, when strict Wolffianism was dissolved into 'popular philosophy', partly under the influence of British
philosophy. Epistemologically speaking, people generally remained
content with a not too subtle distinction between *a priori* rational
knowledge and *a posteriori* sensory knowledge, and understood the
latter as various kinds of knowledge to be distinguished according to
fields of knowledge. But, in connection with the reversal of religious
and metaphysical interests, there was also a development of new interests in aesthetics and anthropology which referred to new experience
and made new forms of experience possible. On the one hand, even
towards the end of the Enlightenment the experience of the beautiful
took on an almost religious dignity; on the other hand, the question
'What is man?', which replaced classical metaphysical problems, was
also to be answered empirically. In all these debates, however, there
was recourse, as with the entire Enlightenment, to experience not in
the sense of so-called pure perception, but in the sense of a structured
experience of the world and of life. 'As everyday experience shows',
and also 'As reason and experience show', was a favourite trope in
argument.

At the same time, Kant recognized the significance of epistemological empiricism as a way to scepticism. Kant, who contrasted dogmatic rationalism and sceptical empiricism with a now classical distinction, tried to surmount this fatally and schematically fixed alternative by means of a critique which relied on the limitation of experiential and of rational knowledge. On the basis of a distinction between the thing-in-itself and mere appearance for us, scientific experience was reduced to experience, and experience to sensory perception; in the process, sensory experience was presented as being always regulatively ordered by the operation of the functions of understanding. In addition, this epistemological notion of experience, which was expressly stated but not unambiguously explained, Kant offered other conceptions of experience in which it was not presented merely as the simple reception of sensory material. Accordingly, he emphasized the necessity of a pragmatic experience of the world, and conceived the history of reason as a history of reason and experience.

## THE REALIZATION OF REASON AND EXPERIENCE

The historical process of revelation of reason and experience which found its initial culmination in the Enlightenment, implied a material problem which is relevant to present-day requests for a new Enlightenment: How does reason become critical (through experience and in regard to experience)? In this case, instead of starting from the Enlightenment discussion of reason and experience, we would have to start from the Enlightenment itself as a specific experience of reason and a specific actualization of experience by reason. To what extent is reason only a mere extension of experience, so to speak only a reproduction of the encounter with reality on a higher plane? To what extent is experience itself made relevant for criticism through a commitment of reason? As one might suppose already happened in antiquity, in the so-called transition from myth to *logos,* reason discovered itself anew in the transition from the Middle Ages to the modern age, in the revaluation of the relationship between reason and faith. The Enlightenment came into being by discovering its nature as critical reason through the criticism of un-reason. Whatever is present or potential in human reason since it has existed, reason becomes conscious of itself only in an historical process and through incalculable experience. To that extent, reason depends on historical experience, and on experience and self-experience, whether the historically acquired or enacted potential of reason subsequently persists relatively identically in history, or shows itself to be changeable and transient. Reason, however, can certainly be conceived not only as (so to speak extended) experience. Reason is also, and perhaps even primarily, perception—but discriminating perception of what is experienced in various ways and as various. In comparison of experiences, reason rises above experience in order (with the aid of other experiences) to test and order that experience; reason has to be able to differentiate and negate. To that extent at least, it takes up an independent standpoint in relation to experience.

If reason is essentially critical reason, and is only primarily exercised as such, and also through criticism of reason itself, then the question of how reason becomes critical cannot be answered by general recourse to experience. Which experiences therefore does Enlightenment make possible as criticism? There are probably critical experiences, that is, crises in the experience of reality, which lead to the experience and grasp of the possibility of criticism. But the fact that such unexpected spurs to criticism may be realized by reason as possibilities of reason, can only be grounded in reason itself, and in the will of reason for itself. But the way in which this will to reason is itself enacted is ultimately located in human freedom to reason.[1]

*Translated by John Griffiths*

## Notes

1. On the beginnings of criticism, see W. Schneiders, *Die wahre Aufklärung. Zum Selbstverständnis der deutschen Aufklärung* (Freiburg & Munich, 1974). On Christian Thomasius, see W. Schneiders, *Naturrecht und Liebesethik, Zur Geschichte der praktischen Philosophie im Hinblick auf Christian Thomasius* (Hildesheim & New York, 1971).

Jan Hulshof

# The Modernist Crisis: Alfred Loisy and George Tyrrell

OPPONENTS within the Church were the first to attach the label 'Modernism' to the reformist trends which came to notice here and there in the Church at the beginning of this century. This term was meant to convey that the appeal to contemporary experience against established values and institutions was suspect. The term soon came into general use to describe what was going on in the circles that gathered around the French priest-exegete, Alfred Loisy (1857-1940), the Irish Jesuit of Anglican origin and publicist, George Tyrrell (1861-1909), the cosmopolitan Baron Friedrich von Hügel (1852-1925) and some Italian priests such as Ernesto Buonaiuti (1881-1946), Salvatore Minocchi (1869-1943), and others.[1]

These people did not represent a clearly defined movement. There was no common programme, although von Hügel provided a kind of liaison between several of them and there was a certain recognition of common experiences. But these experiences can only be brought together under one very general denominator: the feeling that religious, cultural and scientific authenticity was being strangled by the heavy pressure of established institutions and traditions.

## THE ECCLESIASTICAL CLIMATE DURING THE SECOND HALF OF THE NINETEENTH CENTURY

Modernism was a crisis of the Catholic intelligentsia. The second half of the nineteenth century was the time when scientific specialization began to penetrate the Catholic Church in a hesitant but irresistible way. There were de Rossi (archeology), von Döllinger (patrology), von Hefele (history of the Councils) and Duchesne (history of the liturgy and ancient ecclesiastical institutions), to mention only a few names. To see the upheaval caused by Duchesne in France when he unsettled the apostolic origin of the French dioceses in his *Fastes Episcopaux* was enough to make one guess the shock that was going to be caused by the critical study of the Bible. Few were prepared for the situation. In 1902 Albert Houtin published a merciless analysis of the pitiful state in which biblical studies were at that time.[2] He showed how for years the ecclesiastical authorities tried to row against the current with censure and condemnation. Only the most astute realized that there was but one way out. Somebody like Lagrange, for instance, was convinced that nothing but an unprejudiced attitude towards scientific methods could offer any hope in the long run. At the time everybody felt that historical criticism provoked a crisis, a kind of swing situation: at one end one seemed to reach the rock-bottom of historical facts while at the other end one was left in mid-air. As soon as historical criticism opens up new insights into the past, it reduces the absolute claims of today's established certainties.

The rise of historical criticism was but one aspect of a whole cultural trend which was characterized by an increasing appeal to one's own conscience, freedom of research, freedom of expression and freedom of religion. The sharp condemnations of liberalism in official ecclesiastical statements drove many Catholics into a kind of cultural isolation. It is true that Leo XIII brought about some relaxation of the tension through his encyclical *Libertas* and his rallying policies. But the attempt to make the Church meet the 'spirit of the age' was rather a matter of pragmatic considerations than of some inner sensitivity to the ideals of 1789 and 1848. In any case, towards the end of Leo XIII's pontificate the forces of intransigence again gained the upper hand.

In theology, too, a rift developed between contemporary experience and ecclesiastical language. As long as metaphysical categories determined the general view of the world, religious experience could obviously express itself in such concepts. But when this world-view was critically analyzed, this changed. There was a growing conviction that contact with the divine was not a speculative matter but could only take place through experience in the practice of living religiously and morally. Theoretically, the subjective and relativising approach did not seem to exceed the demands of the truth. Obviously Catholic theologians tried to find an answer to the questions raised by the age of enlightenment and romanticism. The Tübingen School, however, passed its zenith in the second half of the nineteenth century and Cardinal Newman remained on his lonely eminence. In general, theological productivity showed little creativity. Preference tended to hark back to medieval models of thought. Kleutgen brought out his *Theologie der Vorzeit* and his *Philosophie der Vorzeit*. Neo-scholasticism became increasingly a safe fortress in a period when Christianity apparently had to face a generally hostile mood.[3]

This was the climate in which Modernism sprang up. In what follows we shall trace the way in which two of its leading figures, Loisy and Tyrrell, expressed and coped with the tension between contemporary experience and traditional values and certainties, each in his own way.

### ALFRED LOISY

Loisy's plea for experience was first of all for this experience in the field of historical criticism. He knew that this was only one aspect of the problem, but it was a genuine aspect which, moreover, was not unimportant from the pastoral and political point of view. Over against the many who kept silent because they were afraid, he put himself forward as one who spoke up because he was afraid that his silence would scandalize those who were aware of the situation. 'A chacun sa clientèle'.[4] If Catholicism was not to degenerate into an obscure reactionary sect, it would have to take the scientific experience of responsible criticism seriously.

One feature of this experience is that it cannot be theoretically disproved. 'A mountain of syllogisms is powerless over against one grain of sand in nature'.[5] This does not mean that every experience is definitive; it remains open to correction but only in the field of the experience itself. 'A hypothesis which cannot stand up against the facts is finished and no further discussion *via* other authorities is required'.[6]

This is why Loisy found any ecclesiastical tutelage unacceptable. It was not a matter of self-sufficiency but of authenticity. 'The primary condition for scientific work is freedom. The first duty of the scientist, whether Catholic or not, is sincerity'.[7] The historian is not allowed to bridge the gap between past and present by means of dogmatic prejudice or tendentious actualization. The historian of religion would show how closely religious experience is interwoven with a historical context from which it cannot be unravelled without damaging the whole. What this meant in the concrete was explained by Loisy in 1902 in his controversy with Harnack who, with A. Sabatier, was a spokesman for liberal Protestant theology.[8] Harnack and Sabatier tried to prize the intimate experience of the faith itself out of the historical forms in which it was expressed. In his *L'Evangile et l'Eglise* Loisy showed that the basic experiences of the Gospel in no way displayed such a timeless and interiorized character. They are inseparably inter-

woven with a previous history and a historical aftermath, with the
Israelite belief in God and the eschatological expectations of the Jews
on the one hand and the ecclesiastical tradition on the other. Any
attempt to extract a timeless inner religious experience from this whole
in order to present it as the essence of Christianity is, according to
Loisy, bound to expose Christianity to the peril of evaporation. 'When
one reduces Christianity to one single point, one single truth, which
Jesus' consciousness would have perceived and revealed, one protects
religion far less from every kind of attack than is thought, since one
robs it practically of every contact with reality, all historical support
and rational guarantee'.[9] In this sense, Loisy finds the harmony between liberal theology and historical criticism suspect from the start.
There is no conflict because there is no encounter.[10] Given the gap
between the historical context of the Gospel and that of our own days,
man clearly has to rely on interpretation. The way in which the Gospel
continues to operate in the Christian tradition shows that 'the whole
Gospel was bound up with a view of the world and of history which is
no longer ours, and that the whole Gospel, and not only its assumed
essence, was not inseparably linked with it'.[11] This tradition was already fully at work within the New Testament itself. 'Whatever one
thinks theologically of tradition, whether one trusts it or suspects it,
Christ is only known by, through and in the oldest Christian tradition.
In other words, Christ cannot be separated from his work, and one tries
to do something that is only half-possible when one wants to determine
the nature of Christianity according to the pure Gospel of Jesus regardless of the tradition, as if the mere idea of a Gospel without tradition
was not already in flagrant contradiction with the factual situation
which is being subjected to criticism'.[12] Thus the historically changing
interpretations of the Gospel must be seen in the light of this active
ecclesiastical tradition. For Loisy, the defence of the plasticity of
Catholicism goes hand in hand with his defence of historical criticism.

   Although a number of kindred minds found Loisy's reply to Harnack
brilliant, others found the medicine worse than the disease. Loisy expressed their objections in his *Autour d'un petit livre*. If one puts the
Church's teaching and dogmas so firmly into their historical perspective, what remains of the revelation? 'Aren't we denying that the
dogma is the truth, that it is revealed, unalterable, guaranteed by God
in the Church's teaching, when we accept that it was formulated by
men, has constantly to rely on interpretation, is constantly in a state of
flux and can hardly be guaranteed today when in all likelihood it will
change again tomorrow?'[13]

   This kind of question assumes that the form of the revelation shares
in God's eternity. But is not all human knowledge necessarily con-

ditioned and marked by history? Revelation is not an infringement of the structure of our human knowledge, no more than the historical form of the revelation is an encroachment on God's transcendence. It is true that theology talks about a natural and a supernatural knowledge of God, but this distinction is pretty abstract and difficult to work with in the concrete history of religion.[14] So Loisy has no difficulty in describing the beginning of the revelation in terms of man's growing consciousness. 'What at some given moment was the beginning of the revelation was the perception—however rudimentary one thinks this was—of the relationship which must exist between man, conscious of himself, and God, present behind the world of phenomena'.[15] The images and concepts which built up religious communication were not themselves revealed. They already existed in the human mind before there was any question of revelation.[16] The dogmas were not truths that fell out of the sky,[17] but ways of interpreting the faith that are related to a changing cultural and philosophical context, and can only be understood from that angle. But where can we find some kind of constant in the history of the revelation among so many variables? According to Loisy there is no way of pinning down such a constant in pure and simple terms. It is rather a matter of a fundamental unity of spirit which pervades and links the three levels of revelation: the pre-reflective consciousness, the level of assertion in religious communication, and the speculative level. This spirit finds expression in historically-created forms but at the same time transcends them. 'The unchanging meaning is not the meaning which, taken strictly, is the result of the letter, that is, of the specific form which the truth has assumed in the mind of those who have come to some formulation; nor does the unchanging meaning lie in the several ways of interpreting which succeed each other as the need occurs; it lies buried in the common ground of both which cannot be expressed in human language by some definition which would be adequate for its object and would suffice for all time'.[18]

## GEORGE TYRRELL

While Loisy's plea for experience shows above all a longing for scientific freedom and authenticity, Tyrrell's reveals a wider context. He is above all concerned with more room for religious authenticity. Official ecclesiastical documents easily link this tendency with disobedience and self-sufficiency, but Tyrrell sees the one true sin in that people delegate their own inalienable responsibility to external authorities. Thus he wrote to Henri Bremond in 1901: 'Our whole life, in the pulpit, in the confessional, in the parlour or when we chair a meeting, forces us to play a part, to speak in the name of the church, or the society, or of a system and tradition which are *ours,* like the clothes we wear, but are not *us.* At most we defend some thesis put before us by somebody else. I begin to believe that the one real sin is suicide or the fact that one is not oneself'.[19]

Among the many things in the Church which prevent people from being themselves theology plays a part which is peculiarly its own. In 1899 Tyrrell published an article, 'The Relation of Theology to Devotion', in which he analyzed the alienating effect of theology.[20] The article was a turning-point in Tyrrell's life. At first he had seen the *depositum fidei* as the first inspired chapter of theology. Insight in historical development forced him to resort to a constantly more elastic theory of doctrinal development in order to enable him to maintain the identity of the content of revelation in the course of history. In the end he had to ask himself whether it wasn't more obvious to understand the *depositum fidei* as a 'spirit' or 'principle' rather than as a 'form of sound words'. But a certain untouchability of the development of theology and doctrine had always predominated. Then, in 1899, he saw that he had grossly overrated the importance of theology. Does the theological tradition really have such a mediating function between the original revelation and today's believer? Is the question of the continuity of this theological development really so important? Does theology constitute the *lex credendi?* Is ecclesiastical doctrine as the deposit of such a theological development perhaps the *lex credendi?* If not, where should we look for it?

To start with, it seems that in the secular sectors of life, too, theoretical knowledge lags somehow behind the knowledge that comes from practical experience. 'It must further be noticed that on the whole the backwoodsman has a truer knowledge of nature than a mere acquaintance with a science-manual could ever impart'.[21] This danger of overrating scientific knowledge, which indeed has an important function to fulfil, is still greater when it is a matter of speaking about God. According to Tyrrell the importance of philosophical concepts lies rather in criticism than in the positive content. They can protect the faith from an uncritical trust in anthropomorphic presentations, however necessary these may be.[22]

God, says Tyrrell, did not reveal himself to the wise and the intelligent, the philosophers and the theologians, but to children, peasants and fishermen. He spoke the language of the *profanum vulgus.* The supervisory function of the Church does not consist in having to develop the revelation. It simply must protect this revelation and preserve it in its authenticity.[23] This concrete prophetic language of revelation, as the first who listened to it understood it, is the *depositum fidei* in the true sense. That is why devotion needs no theological approval. Anyone trying all the same to look for such a theoretical legitimation may well find an empty tomb, like Mary Magdalen: 'They have taken away my Lord, and I do not know where they have laid him'.[24] But this does not, of course, mean either that devotion holds sway over theology. Both are subject to the authority of the concrete language of the revelation. In case a conflict arises between the two the matter is not settled by rational argument but by the lived Gospel. 'If certain forms of prayer and devotion are undoubtedly Catholic, no theology that proves them unreal or ridiculous can be sound. If any analysis of the act of faith or charity or of contrition, would make such acts seem exceedingly difficult to realize, we know at once the analysis must be faulty, since the simplest and most ignorant Catholics make such acts easily and abundantly. If any theology of grace or predestination or of the sacraments would make men pray less, or watch less, or struggle less, then we may be perfectly sure that such theology is wrong'.[25]

According to Tyrrell, then, theology has no immediate hermeneutical function. Theology is not a (methodical-reflexive) element in the process of understanding the revealed truth but rather a critical reflexion on the irreplaceable peculiar character of this process which does not operate *via* theology but *via* religion. Theology and religion are not related to each other as the reflexive and the symbolic form of the same truth but rather as art criticism is related to art and grammar to the living language. Art criticism is not a higher form of art, it is in no way a form of art; in the same way theology is not a higher form of faith, it is in no way a form of faith. But just as under certain conditions art criticism can serve art, so can theology under certain conditions serve the faith.[26]

In 1907 Tyrrell pursued this line of thought in his article on revelation and quite explicitly applied its conclusions to the matter of ecclesiastical doctrine and dogma. The Church's teaching and dogma are not in themselves theology, and therefore need not satisfy the criteria of theological rationality. Neither are they a form of revelation. 'Dogmatic decisions are neither theological nor revelational in value, but merely protective of revelation'.[27] Such decisions should therefore not be judged by their truthfulness but by their opportuneness. 'What is perfectly true may create a false impression; what is perfectly false may create a true impression. Relative to a certain mentality the greater truth may be the greater lie'.[28]

In this sense, both theology and dogma only fulfil a certain external function in the process of making the revelation one's own. Tyrrell greatly reduced the hermeneutical function of a historical-institutional intermediate agency. Yet, some such mediation is necessary for what was directly revealed to John was not directly revealed to us: 'For us the Revelation of St John is but the record of an experience; for him it was an experience. St Stephen saw the Heavens opened; we are but told that he saw them opened. To him they were revealed, to us it is only revealed that they were revealed'.[29]

Experiences cannot be reproduced. It is true that one can meet with a mental impression which was part of a classic experience and recognize it as such: 'In that impression we still hold one element of that great collective religious experience. From it we can judge of the nature of the other elements, aided, moreover, by some measure of like experience within ourselves—much as a man in love will to some extent rightly interpret the self-utterances of some heroic and classical lover, even though his own passion falls short of that standard in strength and purity'.[30]

Revelation can therefore become an experience for us when in a process of inner recognition the prophetic word is assimilated as a word of our own, as the explanation of our own existence. For Tyrrell therefore the recognition of the Word does not come about so much through an historical-cultural process as through an inner-personal event. 'In other words, the teaching from outside must evoke a revelation in ourselves; the experience of the prophet must become experience for us. It is to this evoked revelation that we answer by the act of Faith, recognizing it as God's word in us and to us. Were it not already written in the depths of our being, where the spirit is rooted in God, we could not recognize it'.[31]

## LOISY AND TYRRELL

Even this very summary reproduction of the ideas of Loisy and Tyrrell shows that one can hardly speak of *the* Modernist idea about revelation and experience. There are some remarkable differences. Loisy is more concerned with the problem of the historical distance between the world of experience of the Gospel and that of modern man. That is why for Loisy the necessity of a historical-institutional mediation is prominent. Precisely because of its institutional character the Church transcends the limited scope of the individual's experience. 'Only an enduring society, a church, can maintain the equilibrium between the tradition which preserves the heritage of the acquired truth and the unceasing labour of human reason in order to adjust the old truth to the new conditions of thought and science'.[32]

In Tyrrell, this distance in time is not so prominent. He thinks that the language of the Gospel with its concrete images enjoys a kind of universal intelligibility. This intelligibility is barely affected by the fact that the Gospel is tied to a certain time and place.[33] Tyrrell is therefore less interested in an historico-institutional mediation between the prophetic experience and present-day experience, and attaches more importance to a more sacramental-symbolic mediation which is more readily explained in anthropological concepts.[34] Tyrrell is also more fascinated than Loisy by the mysterious correspondence between man's deepest longings and the Word of God who, indeed, comes into his own (*in propria venit*). Because Tyrrell is less laboriously involved in the historical warp and woof of the revelation, he brings out more clearly the transcending and normative character of the evangelical revelation. Loisy sees in this tendency of Tyrrell's a certain analogy with Protestant ideas of the absoluteness of the revelation of the Gospel.[35] These ideas do not appeal to him. He holds that to absolutize a specific experience is 'to undervalue the social character of the human being and the profound physical, intellectual and moral solidarity which exists between every individual and the rest of mankind, past, present and future'.[36] Catholicism means the implicit denial that such an individual 'punctual' revelation can be absolutely sufficient and unchangeable.[37]

Loisy and Tyrrell are very far apart indeed, although they came into history together under the general description of Modernism, saw together their ideas condemned in 1907, and were shortly after together driven out of the ecclesiastical community. The questions they left behind were not the same either. For Tyrrell the vital question was that of the constitutive importance of tradition and dogma in the hermeneutical process. For Loisy it was the issue of the scope of historical criticism, its presuppositions and its range. For, seen as an autonomous, ontological reconstruction of reality itself, the science of history leaves barely room for the experience of a transcendent self-revelation of God in history. Because of their dedicated concentration on these problems people like Maurice Blondel and Friedrich von Hügel in a sense grew out of the immediate statements of the problem of the Modernist crisis.[38]

*Translated by Theo Westow*

## Notes

1. R. Aubert has given an extensive survey of the literature in his *Histoire de l'Eglise,* vol. X, ch. X (1974).

2. A. Houtin, *La question biblique chez les catholiques de France au XIXe siècle* (Paris, 1902).

3. Cf. B. Welte, *Zum Strukturwandel der Theologie im 19. Jahrhundert:* id., *Auf der Spur des Ewigen* (Freiburg, 1965), p. 399.

4. Alfred Loisy, *Autour d'un petit livre* (second ed., Paris, 1903), Avant-propos, p. XXXII.

5. Ibid., p. 114: 'Une montagne de syllogismes ne peut rien contre un grain de sable en nature'.

6. Ibid., p. 36: 'Celle qui ne tient pas devant les faits est condamnée par là et n'a pas besoin d'être discutée autrement'.

7. Ibid., Avant-propos, p. X: 'La première condition du travail scientifique est la liberté. Le premier devoir du savant, catholique ou non, est la sincérité'.

8. The controversy refers to A. von Harnack's *Das Wesen des Christen-thums* (Leipzig, 1900).

9. Alfred Loisy, *L'Evangile et l'Eglise* (2nd enl. ed., Paris, 1903), Intr., p. XXXI: 'En réduisant le christianisme à un seul point, à une seule vérité que la conscience de Jésus aurait perçue et révélée, on protège bien moins qu'on ne croit la religion contre toute attaque, attendu qu'on la prive à peu près de tout contact avec la réalité, de tout appui dans l'histoire, et de toute garantie devant la raison'.

10. Ibid., Intr., p. XII.

11. Ibid., p. 100: 'L'Evangile tout entier était lié à une conception du monde et de l'histoire qui n'est plus la nôtre, et c'est L'Evangile tout entier, non seulement sa prètendue essence, qui n'y était pas lié "inséparablement" '.

12. Ibid., Intr. p. XXI: 'Quoi que l'on pense, théologiquement, de la tradition, que l'on s'y fie ou que l'on s'en défie, on ne connaît le Christ que par la tradition, à travers la tradition, dans la tradition chrétienne primitive. Autant dire que le Christ est inséparable de son oeuvre, et que l'on tente une entreprise qui n'est qu'à moitié réalisable, quand on veut définir l'essence du christianisme d'après le pur Evangile de Jésus, en dehors de la tradition, comme si cette seule idée de l'Evangile sans la tradition n'était pas en contradiction flagrante avec l'état du fait qui est suomis à la critique'.

13. Loisy, *Autour,* p. 189: 'N'est-ce pas nier que le dogme soit vrai, qu'il soit révélé, qu'il soit immunable, qu'il soit autorisé de Dieu dans l'enseignement de l'Eglise, puisqu'il a été formulé par des hommes, qu'il a besoin constamment d'être interprété, qu'il est dans un flux perpétuel, et qu'il ne peut pas être bien garanti pour aujourd'hui, s'il a toute chance d'être changé demain?'

14. Ibid., pp. 194f.

15. Ibid., p. 196: 'Ce qui fut, à un moment donné, le commencement de la révélation, a été la perception, si rudimentaire qu'on la suppose, du rapport qui doit exister entre l'homme, conscient de lui-même, et Dieu présent derrière le monde phénoménal'.

16. Ibid., p. 196.

17. Loisy, *L'Evangile*, pp. 202f.: 'Les conceptions que l'Eglise présente comme des dogmes révélés ne sont pas des vérités tombées du ciel et gardées par la tradition religieuse dans la forme précise où elles ont paru d'abord'.

18. Loisy, *Autour*, pp. 201f.: 'Le sens qui ne change pas n'est pas celui qui résulte précisément de la lettre, c'est-à-dire la forme particulière que la vérité prenait dans l'esprit de ceux qui ont libellé la formulé; il n'est pas davantage dans la forme particulière des interprétations qui se succèdent selon le besoin; il est dans leur fond commun, impossible, à exprimer en langage humain, par une définition adéquate à son objet et suffisante pour les siècles des siècles'.

19. *Lettres de George Tyrrell à Henri Bremond*, ed., trans. and annotated by A. Louis-David (Paris, 1971), p. 96: 'Notre vie tout entière, en chaire, au confessional, au parloir ou quand nous présidons une réunion, nous oblige à jouer un rôle; à parler au nom de l'Eglise ou de la Compagnie ou d'un système et d'une tradition qui sont *nôtres,* comme sont nos vêtements, mais qui ne sont pas *nous.* Tout au plus défendons-nous une thèse qui nous est proposée par quelqu'un d'autre. Je commence à penser que le seul péché véritable est le suicide ou le fait de ne pas être soi-même'.

20. The article appeared in *The Month* (Nov. 1899) and was incorporated under a new title, 'Lex ordandi, lex credendi' in 1907 in a collection entitled, *Through Scylla and Charybdis* (London, 1907), pp. 85-105.

21. Ibid., p. 88.

22. Ibid., pp. 91f.

23. Ibid., p. 95.

24. Ibid., p. 100.

25. Ibid., pp. 104f.

26. Ibid., p. 105.

27. Ibid., p. 293.

28. Ibid., p. 299.

29. Ibid., p. 268.

30. Ibid., pp. 291f.

31. Ibid., p. 305.

32. Loisy, *L'Evangile*, p. 216: 'Une société durable, une Eglise peut seule maintenir l'équilibre entre la tradition qui conserve l'héritage de la vérité acquise, et le travail incessant de la raison humaine pour adapter la vérité ancienne aux états nouveaux de la pensée et de la science'.

33. George Tyrrell, *Christianity at the Crossroads* (London, 1909), p. 211.

34. Ibid., pp. 265f.: 'The Spirit of Jesus uttered in the Church, in the Gospel, in the sacraments, is apprehended by his followers, not as a doctrine but as a personal influence, fashioning the soul to its own divine nature. It is impossible for spirit or personality to find adequate expression in terms of another order of experience. It is by a sort of internal sympathy that we read the personality of another out of the meagre shorthand of words and acts and gestures, and only so far as we are latently capable of realising a similar personality in ourselves'.

35. See Loisy's review of one of Tyrrell's books (the French translation of *Through Scylla and Charybdis*) in *Revue d'histoire et de litt. rel.*, new series, II, 1911, p. 609.

36. Alfred Loisy, *Quelques lettres sur des questions actuelles et sur des*

*événements récents* (Ceffonds, 1908), pp. 43f.: 'Mais je crois aussi que l'inclination générale des protestants, même les plus remarquables par l'ouverture de l'esprit et la générosité du coeur, à considérer l'individu comme un tout indépendant, la foi personnelle comme une religion complète, l'expérience de chacun comme une révélation totale en soi, méconnaît le caractère social de l'être humain et la solidarité foncière, je veux dire physique, intellectuelle et morale, qui existe entre chaque individu et le reste de l'humanité, passée, présente, et future'.

37. Loisy, *Autour,* p. 206.

38. Cf. the important exchange between Loisy and Blondel. See J. Hulshof, *Wahrheit und Geschichte. Alfred Loisy zwischen Tradition und Kritik* (Essen, 1973), pp. 137-81.

Dietmar Mieth

# What Is Experience?

CONCEPT OR ROOT-WORD?

THE SIMPLEST meaning of 'experience' seems to be that man re-
ceives impressions which give rise to perceptions. In the active sense
one can also seek out impressive situations and gather impressions,
thereby opening out the world of planned perception and observation.
But even the simplest perception of an object demands that we differentiate it from other objects, thus establishing its relationship to other
perceptions. Hence, right from the start, philosophy defines experience
in the sense of the differentiation and integration of perceptions and
memories. Ever since Aristotle experience has required the ability to
think in abstract terms and is directly related to theory. One can deflect
experience from theory, but then it is impossible to formulate synthetic
concepts and judgments. This led Kant to link experience (in the most
empirical sense) to the categorical operation of reason. However, in so
doing, experience also becomes a problem of the relationship between
the general and the particular which is Hegel's especial concern. To
him, experience is essentially the historical movement of spirit, which
brings him finally to the concept. Thought is not distinguished from
experience; rather, it gives an experience of thinking, not only a
thought of experience. Phenomenology poses the subsequent question:
how do I experience the experience?[1]

'To endure' an experience, 'to make' an experience; experience as
perception and abstract inference; the greatest particularity on the one
hand and the most comprehensive generalization on the other—these
are all problems which must be contended with in any concept of
experience. Experience has many meanings, which can only be defined
according to its specific geographical location. Any attempt to reduce

40

the word 'experience' to the generalized level of a concept by means of an unequivocal formula would thus be a rather hopeless undertaking. We may thus assume that what the various different regional concepts of experience have in common is a kind of 'root-word' (or image, or even metaphor if you prefer) for the complex mode of the origins of human insight as well as for a spiritual movement which interprets this mode in a specifically historical way. The complexity of this mode consists in the fact that in it recur all the dimensions of human perception; cognition, observation, experience, insight, understanding, and so on.

A little of the complexity of the root word 'experience' becomes apparent when two different generations are in dispute, both claiming 'experience' for themselves, one in the sense of tradition, the other in the sense of a radical novelty. One generation wants to see experience as something constant, while the other wants the freedom to make it in the first place. If we regard experience as the root-word of contemporary spirituality, we are almost certainly interpreting it in the experimental sense of the word. This is by no means self-evident. Had 'experience' been adopted twenty years ago, it would certainly have been done in the sense of salvaging tradition. Experience was nothing for the inexperienced; ''experience'' was the concern of those who 'had it' and not of those who only wanted to 'have it'. This has now changed fundamentally.

'Experience' as a mode of adaptation and experience as a mode of inability to adapt, of the possibility of falsifying experimentation in life, in the sciences and in the arts. However the meaning is shifted it includes a shift in the criteria of interpretation. The root-word 'experience' is historical; it can only be grasped by distinguishing between the various meanings. In this way we can also ascertain just where the aggressive point of this meaning lies today and what we expect in insisting on experience. Our aim is therefore to examine these many different meanings and to sort out those which are particularly emphasized today.

If we are seeking a definition based on precedent, we may subscribe to an account given by H. Rombach which aims rather to indicate the problem than to 'define' it: 'Experience is that mode of perception which refers to given facts and circumstances and presents them as though belonging to the same context and thus having an objective appearance . . . (Experience) is based on sensory perception (direct cognition) but is never limited to this. Rather it draws ''conclusions,'' ''develops'' laws, ''goes back'' to the motives or places various other interpretations on data previously gained under the dominance of specific interpretations'.[2] Today we must also proceed from the assumption that experiences differ structurally in accordance with the area of experience.

This also means a structural independence of "religious" experience as a specific experience of experience which simultaneously establishes itself as the area within which all other experiences are gained. In the last analysis the problem of religious experience is to experience this, 'freely' given the historical reserve of the transmission of the faith, and hence given a certain reserve towards fundamental experiences. In addition, the law seems to make the distinction that the achievement of experiences is linked to the extension and intensification of experiences.[3] Experience in general and the sphere of religious experience in particular are only alive when open-ended. An attempt will be made in the remainder of this article to elucidate those structures of experience which are also important for an explicit discussion about the experience of faith.

## COMPLEXITY OF EXPERIENCE

### Dimensions and types of experience

The root-word 'experience' exists first and foremost in a totally commonplace dimension. We speak, for example, of an experienced pilot, by which we mean someone who has mastered a particular skill, namely flying. It is not enough just to know the relevant facts, for it is precisely the difference between knowledge and ability that is in question. The Indo-Germanic root of the German and Romance nuances of meaning of 'erfahren' (experiri)—'to explore by travelling' and 'to acquire experimentally'—already indicates that the question of experience does not exist independently of the individual. According to the German version, the experienced man is 'the travelled man' who knows the world not just by hearsay, but because he has been there, has participated, suffered with his fellow men, taken part in the action. According to the Romance version the 'expert' or 'peritus' gathers his insights by means of trial, attempt, error and confirmation. Experience in this sense cannot simply be transferred to another person; it cannot be transmitted in the way that we communicate something 'objectively', but rather in the way we live together. The transmission of experiences gained demands a living community regardless of the fact that identical experiences can be made on the basis of identical conditions, though this does not necessarily apply.

In recognizing the subjective dependence of experience it has sometimes been seen as the central element of all experience. In thus emphasizing the subjective 'origins', the aspect of social transmission has on occasion been forgotten.[4]

Instead of stressing the individual 'experience', we may equally stress the pragmatic character of the everyday variety of experience. In reality, this daily experience is relevant in the sense of a suspended doubt and hence of self-evident participation. For this reason, it sometimes has difficulty in adapting to the growing complexity of modern life. In addition, the subjective and practical aspects of experience are by no means sufficient to be hailed as the 'solution' to complex problems. Anyone who is only competent in the sense of this everyday dimension of experience would prefer to distance himself from any sphere in which he cannot participate with 'experience' and lives in a state of self-effacement: the everyday form of wisdom.

The attempt to exclude subjectivity and pragmatism from experience—we shall come to the social transmission later—brings us to that sphere of experience known generally as 'empirical', in which the most important elements are detailed perception, 'objective' observation and evaluation. In this sense, experience becomes the basis for all scientific studies orientated towards the natural sciences, and man acquires a wide range of artificial 'sensors', from the microscope to the space probe, which extend his sphere of observation enormously. The criticism that empirical observations are dependent on the relative precision of the instruments, on the given axiomatics and on the impossibility of 'pure' induction, is not applicable to the extent that the empiricist is fully aware of the necessity to recognize and exclude pre-requisites.

Another attempt to 'objectify' experience leads to the 'hermeneutical' aspect of the elucidation of experience. This is more important not only for the arts, but for linking experience to faith and revelation. For no one would wish to claim that psychological or sociological religious empiricism led to faith or disclosed the real meaning of revelation. The hermeneutics of symbols seems to be more promising in this respect.[5]

We do not wish to go into the theoretical issues at this point, but it is nevertheless of theoretical significance to differentiate between 'empiricism' and 'experience'.[6] J. Mouroux has suggested describing the three dimensions of experiences (including the everyday one) as 'empirical', 'experimental' and 'experiential'.[7] This differentiation is perhaps not entirely apposite since in some languages the word 'empiricism' suggests a scientific rather than a naive dimension of experience, and because the experimental character is present in all experiences, although in different ways. For example, religious experience has also been described as *cognitio experimentalis* (Bonaventure), and in the sphere of daily experience we assume right from the outset that being moulded by trial and error is a symptomatic part of our lives. As far as the third, experiential dimension of experience is concerned, we may however follow Mouroux. It is only with this dimension that the synthetic powers of the human spirit are fully introduced into the discussion. Hence in the following we shall be dealing chiefly with the experiential mode of experience.

## Experience as process and event

Experience seems to obtain when all possibilities of a specific skill have been mastered. But there is also evidence of experience in the sense of the unique event or impression, of the direct encounter, of intuitive comprehension. To this extent experience as something particular, as a 'concretissimum' is openly opposed to experience as the common denominator and synopsis.

It is precisely this opposition which spurs on the processes of experience. If we try to comprehend the integrating meaning of experience we come across a chain of individual experiences whose continuity in turn depends on the persistent strength of their relationship to a single occurrence—regardless as to whether this in fact exists, empirically speaking. For example, according to his own account in the epistles, Paul's conversion must be regarded more as a process. And yet Acts is not incorrect in drawing this together into one act, into a story which attempts to grasp the overwhelming effect of his encounter with Christ. The layers of Pauline experience and certainty about faith are complex and present problems for exegesis even today. Nevertheless, agreement can exist about a moving occurrence which can best be described as an event because only in this way does the completely surprising, non-causal element of a change become evident. Another example would be the initiation of love. Genetically speaking it is composed of the integration of various individual experiences and it can be the result of a gradual process of which the person concerned is by no means aware at the beginning. On the other hand the initiation of love is also seen as a unique event or happening: love at first sight, 'to fall in love'. Attention is focussed on the moment of surprise when a person is 'suddenly' transposed into a new state of being. In this way experience can be seen as a concentrated process, and as the process of revealing the implications of an event. Neither apparently excludes the other.

## Directness and indirectness

Everything is conveyed—even experience. Were this not so, we should have to claim that experiences only take place in an indeterminate sphere where man moves freely in his little remaining unrestrained freedom. This is sometimes assumed to apply to mystic experiences, but this too has been subject to doubt; at all events man makes the experience he undergoes. Nowadays it is almost a commonplace to say that all experiences are linguistically and socially conveyed. But this act of transmission does not reduce the spontaneity of the experience. Many experiences can be 'explained' without being truly comprehended. If we 'explain' the love between people by pointing out how well they suit each other, we have in no way understood the nature of their love. The transmission of experience, though it can be analyzed especially well by means of the arts, nevertheless conceals the secret of human experience. This secret derives from the arbitrariness of important, formative experiences, which we cannot enforce, know about, or bring about. It is precisely this aspect which, it is sometimes claimed, is the source of the immediacy of experience. Genetic explanations of the way really formative experiences come to be do not affect this immediacy. However, only the person directly affected by the experience will understand its significance. For this reason, arguments are of little use against experiential experiences; nor can they bring about experiential experiences.

### EXPERIENCE OF FAITH: ITS SCOPE AND DEPTH

## Extensity and intensity

Experience of extensity is experience as the basis of the empirically founded judgment of fact. The empirical sciences have to attempt to comprehend all experience as *res extensa*.[8] However, in psychoanalysis and in the various sciences influenced by it this is somewhat different. The intensity of a single experience, its power to impress, plays a greater rôle in psychoanalysis than its repetition, extension and duration. What is important about the intensity of an experience? Is it the experience as a single 'concretissimum' or experience as a whole? Formative experiences are significant because they encompass human existence in its entire scope and depth. A unique characteristic of these important experiences is that they represent what amounts to a concrete generalization; that they may be comprehended as irrevocably concrete on the one hand and as a universal human reality on the other. No one who finds himself immensely attracted to a concrete, unexchangeable, unrepeatable individual would consider this to be a universal condition. And yet he knows that he is undergoing an experience which is universally human and which is known to a great many people. The uniqueness of the experience, in this case linked to a specific meeting or encounter, is not in the least diminished by its universality; that is, by the similarity between the essential features of this experience and those of 'love' as something universal.

As with the experience of love, the concrete universal may also be observed with regard to the experience of trust, which perhaps has as much to do with 'faith' as it has with love. There is a kind of general potential for the experience of trust, known as 'basic trust'. But trust is by no means a self-evident and explicit characteristic in every individual, no more than freedom, the acceptance of self and responsibility. However, without a general potential, man could not pursue his perceptions and actions. Trust is always based on trust, and the more it is actively used, the more powerful it becomes, thus making concrete, absolute trust ever more possible. The concrete, absolute, unique encounter in love and trust; this is also what we find as our reason for faith in the historical and personal uniqueness of Jesus Christ. Nevertheless we claim that no one is excluded from this experience, thereby claiming its universal significance and rightness. We are thus moving indirectly towards questions which need to be theologically thematized. For instance, is the experience of faith an experience which integrates or thwarts all human existence, an overriding (but analogous) or an 'uplifting' (in the dialectical sense) experience? The dispute about revelation and experience should be directed towards these two ways of categorizing the reality of human experience and the specifically Christian content of experience.

## Integration or hindrance?

A central experience must interpret the world in a meaningful way yet at the same time be able to assert itself against the whole world. Once again we are reminded of the phenomena of love and trust. If experience did not consist of integration and hindrance simultaneously, as an occurrence, it would be banal, in conformity and without any further significance. This can be demonstrated with the experience of conscience; if it does not happen, it can be easily manipulated and falls below its own level. The conscience cannot be made valid; rather, it makes itself valid. A formative experience must contain something that makes it valid, against the person actually undergoing it if necessary, even against the whole world. Formative experiences are not universal experiences, but they are decisive.

Occurrences may also be called contrasting experiences. We perceive them clearly as they come and go—we are identical with them, and then we are no longer aware of them at all (which is why the mystics cannot accommodate 'unity' in the mode of experience). So for example, I experience the experience of faith when it overwhelms me (possibly even against me) and forces me to change (my actions, my existence). This is how I experience the experience of faith when it leaves me and I am beset with doubt by its persistent intractability. The coming and going of formative experiences renders their character as occurrences particularly apparent.

Experience as an occurrence—also apparent in the reformational starting point of experience through the challenge of sin—can make it seem as though experience comes 'from above'. It is arbitrary, incalculable and hence cannot be instigated 'from below'. No decision is reached, whether one affirms the source of the occurrence or whether one acknowledges it as 'God' in the context of a tradition of experience, but structurally this perception applies to all central experiences which are thus simultaneously experiences of 'grace'.

Should the central experience therefore be understood above all in terms of its lack of identity with any other kind of experience? It will be seen at a glance that this negative approach is not adequate. An experience can also be discernible to others or involve them. For example: experiential and empirical experience should not be contradictory, indeed attempts have been made to prove that there is no dividing line between them.[9] Pascal adopted this transparency as the basis of his three orders. No matter how varied the dimensions of human experience, there exist structural correspondences between them, for example in their course of development. Hence the pragmatic experience expands from being a divergent experience which cannot be integrated for the very reason that it is refuted. Scientific experience is expanded by means of falsification which forces a reformulation of the horizons of knowledge. And even experiential experience is spurred on through the concrete, contradictory encounter with experiences which cannot be subsumed or classified. This structural correspondence is only possible on the basis of the original unity of experience. This is what Karl Rahner has in mind when he regards transcendental experience as the anonymous point of contact for all religious experience in the form of the concrete encounter.[10]

## Dialectic, analectic, reciprocity

Integration and refutation as the crucial elements of the central experience cannot, however, be brought into complete harmony. In choosing a concept, one must state one's preference for one arrangement or the other. The framework according to which central experiences are given a philosophical definition varies intrinsicly. One of these differences is that between dialectic and analectic. The dialectical form of thought, which has to assume that the reality to be experienced also possesses a dialectical structure, will always see the concrete negation in the central experience. In the forms of dialectical theology too, no matter how little they hold of philosophy, it becomes clear that refutation is one form of the thought of experience.

Some theologians and philosophers, on the other hand, have used as their starting point not so much this contradiction as the tense yet 'inherently critical' unity of formative experience and the general reality of experience. These two, experience and experience, are always relational or reciprocal. This is the position between faith, which implies the reality of experience and reality, which implies faith as the experience. This approach first became widely known through the works of Paul Tillich and comes close to the idea of structural correspondence outlined above. The ultimate source of this relation presupposes a metaphysical groundwork. If existence is thought of as a relational analogy, then one is able to understand the integrating character of formative experiences without levelling out the differences.

### History, practice, meta-practice

After a century of historicism, the historical transmission of experiences is one of the generally accepted tenets of knowledge, with the exception—but only to a certain extent—of the empiricism of the natural sciences. Can one only make certain experiences within the limits of one's period, and can one make certain experiences only within a given period of time? How can experiences be linked together and how do they point towards an integrating horizon?

Now experiences are historical in a dual sense: in the sense of its ultimate originality and in the sense of its continued existence in history. Experiences have so to speak their 'place in our lives' and their *hermeneia* by means of memory and oblivion. Forgetfulness is just as important as memory for the continuity of the live transmission of experience through interpretation, as Nietzsche maintains, for only with the combination of the two does historical experience assume concrete form. Memory and forgetfulness are, however, subject to practical considerations. Continuity of history is the reconstruction of history with a practical view in mind. Historical thought is itself dependent on a theory of action.[11]

Practice constitutes the reflection inherent in historical experience. The bending of the spirit through action and suffering stands in the same relation to experience as the influence of reflection on the mind has to thought. The situational originality of experience comes to fruition in the historical wisdom of experience. The intensity of experience precedes the intensity of a successful experience, but it remains peripheral to man's essential being; the decisive factor is how he permits it to affect him and what he freely makes of it.

In linking experience to practice we are not claiming either that it can be learned or that it could be implemented by training. The technical organization of formative experiences is disputable, and the technical manufacture of experiences by means of manipulative agents such as drugs is an inherent contradiction. In an authentic experience aids, such as fasting once was, must be secondary: that is, they must play a catalytic rather than a casual rôle. However, the fact that formative experiences cannot be manufactured in no way contradicts their practical aspects; for it is through practice that the insight gained acquires a dimension of distance from the action and the effect produced by it. This dimension cannot exist without practice, because it is determined by the nature of cross-reference, while at the same time exceeding what can be achieved by practice. This dimension, without which practice is reduced to mere pragmatism, we call 'meta-practice'.[12] In this sense formative experiences have a meta-physical character, without however being turned into theories.[13] By this we mean, for example, that the practice of love between two individuals, depending on how successful their experience is, opens up possibilities of success otherwise beyond their reach.

Like an analogy of history which points beyond itself there is an analogy of practice which likewise points beyond itself. Experiences are formative so long as they are not definitive but remain open to change and hope. The temporal nature of the occurrence, the limitation of the potential of experience determined by the experiences themselves, must in the final analysis be a positive rather than a negative, limiting factor. To regard experiences as final or definitive is the surest way of reducing their formative power. A 'definitive' experience finds expression in taboos, conventions, and immutable norms and dogmas which make the diminution of the experience almost inevitable. To regard the results of earlier experiences as safely concluded invariably leads to their subsequent refutation. Once love, trust, hope or faith is regarded as a possession to be taken for granted, it is lost. Experience in the form of wisdom knows no end.

## EXPERIENCE TODAY

In our contemporary context, any definition of the concept of experience has to come to terms with the current excessive concentration on experience. It must therefore make distinctions of meaning within the general framework already outlined. We shall attempt to do so by ascertaining the claims made for experience today. This seems to be not so much a case of empiricism versus theory as of claiming a new experience in the sense of a claim to use formative experiences in the sense of assurances of the active transmission of experiences.

## Experience is dead, long live experience!

When experiences diminish, ordering of truth and experience of reality come into conflict. For example, in theology it is traditionally regarded as primarily important that God *exists*, and then that he performs works. However, in the process of the active experience God's existence 'arises' from his works, and from the feeling of trust gained by those who seriously and uncompromisingly surrender themselves to his power.

Theology makes the claim that God 'is'. Experience in the first instance claims to provide an answer to a different question; namely, what happens if I live with God? Thus young people today are leaving the catechism aside, but they do go to Taizé (for example), and then they demand a 'new' catechism. Seen in this light, the death-of-God theology was a claim for the authenticity of the experience of God who could no longer be discerned among theistic conceptions. God's influence is now being sought in new, experimental ways, such as psychology, without having to presuppose God in any previously clearly defined manner. This might seem like a race whose aim is not established before the start, but definitive theology would not permit a search for new horizons. Thus the phenomenon of breaking out in search of experience is characteristic of historical periods, such as the late medieval reaction to scholasticism, which embraced not only mysticism but the practical acceptance of the gospel message too.

Experience is dead—that is, experience which is contained within clearly defined limits and will not admit any new ideas. But experience lives—that is, experience for which the world is full of wonder and misery, which breaks through conventional safeguards and lays itself open to the danger of failure. To see that to make these kinds of claims is not without danger, it is hardly necessary to hear the cries of warning issued by those whose concern is to preserve things as they are. With some 'experience' one may have confidence in the autonomy of freedom in experience. It often re-discovers formative experiences with renewed intensity and reveals the short roots of yesterday's Zeitgeist which had surrounded itself with an aura of eternity, as well as short-lived experiences of today which are not capable of surviving the next trend.

## Ambivalence of experience

In many parts of the world direct experience of the war is waning. Could it be that the new generations will turn this experience into a subject for experiment? The question indicates that the search for new originality of experience is always a dangerous one. It poses a threat to those human experiences which we should desperately like to see reversed. Who could possibly welcome a return to atavisms just for the sake of extending experience? Surely there must be values, insights and indeed 'experiences' which should not be laid open to experiment? Should traditional experiences not be protected against the confusion of a new influx of experiences?

Recourse to experience does not, it seems, resolve the crisis, but it does at any rate offer a diagnosis of crises requiring settlement. In other words, if we wish to resolve a crisis with the help of experience, then we must first of all begin by examining experience.

Experience has become a militant and escapist catch-phrase. It is a reservoir for extreme attitudes, for the active and the mystical delight in experimentation are both confused energies leading finally to a palaver of experiences.

If an experience is to be formative, it must be reflected and controlled.[14] If experience is to achieve anything, it demands progress in the ability to experience. Experience that takes no heed of wisdom is merely on the level of a scream which diagnoses one's own misery. This cry for experience simultaneously indicates the crisis besetting the very thing intended to cure the world—experience itself. Let us take the example of a married couple who no longer experience each other; any attempt to re-create vanished love experiences may be useless in the face of the existing situation. The attempt to reclaim formative experiences thus leads to the death of the said experiences, leaving a genuine need for experience. Experience becomes important precisely when experiences vanish or fade; at other times when actively engaged in the process of experiencing we identify with our experience to such an extent that we scarcely notice it.

What chance is there that this crisis will be resolved? Paradoxically, it is this very crisis which is the pre-requisite for our continually being made aware of experience, that we constantly seek it and live it afresh. With the fading of the love experience, every small indication of any such new encounter will be all the more acutely observed.

Let us try to establish what it is that fades and what we gain from this loss of experience. The ability to experience in fact means to link the ability from experience with the ability for experience. In other words, to see through the complexity of experience, to examine its intensity and to integrate it wholeheartedly. What we need is a flexible approach to experience which is thus continually moving towards its potential wisdom.

### Shock motive or consolation motive?

In her book about experience, D. Sölle recounts how in a situation of the deepest spiritual suffering she found consolation in the biblical

words: 'Have trust in my mercy'.[15] J. B. Metz refers to the orders as
the bearers of experience for the true succession of the Church, and
concludes with the 'shock therapy of the Holy Ghost for the Church as
a whole'.[16] Consolation or shock—what should experience be in the
current move towards greater freedom? The contradiction is surely
insoluble. Not only Sölle and Metz see it this way, so does E.
Fromm.[17] On the contrary, the term 'shock therapy' indicates the
simultaneous presence of 'dangerous' and 'therapeutic' elements. Experience should cure by rousing; it should expose wounds to the restorative draught of critical opinion. The true consolation is a shock at
the same time, as Sölle writes: 'I was at the end and God had torn up
the first draft. He did not offer me consolation like a psychologist
explaining that this was to be foreseen, nor did he offer me the usual
social appeasement. Instead, he threw me face down on the floor'.[18]
The shock of religious experience only gradually assumes the aspect of
a consolation which will refute and overcome all expectations, thereby
'fulfilling' them. A beneficial shock and a genuine consolation are 'occurrences'. They cause a surprise when the ability to experience has
become stultified by the continuity of experience. We should bear in
mind at this juncture that the biblical motive of 'readiness' does not
mean that the shepherds should prevent their sheep from straying by
means of fences, but that one should be fully aware of how things are
moving.

## CONCLUSION

Experience in the realm of faith and revelation 'is' . . . We have not
been able to find any definitive answer to this question because 'experience' itself is not 'definitive' in the sense that it is not bound by any
clearly defined limits, but is open-ended and flexible. Perhaps one
might conclude with a play on words: if openness is historically linked
to the basic structure of experience, then 'revelation' may be said to
signify both a leading into the 'open', at the same time 'revealing', that
is, uncovering and hence by extension removing any protection, pursued only through a continuous dialogue with experience.

*Translated by Sarah Twohig*

## Notes

1. Re. the phenomenology of experience, cf. R. Egenter, *Erfahrung ist Leben* (Munich, 1974); from the more therapeutic point of view, R. D. Laing, *The Politics of Experience* (London, 1967). Historico-philosophical interpretations are offered by: A. S. Kessler, A. Schöpf, C. Wild, 'Erfahrung' in *Handbuch philosophischer Grundbegriffe*, I (Munich, 1973), pp. 373-86. For an elucidation of the concept, cf. W. Brugger, *Philosophisches Wörterbuch* (Freiburg, 1976), article on experience (*Erfahrung*); G. Siewerth, 'Erfahrung' in *THhK*, 3 (1959), pp. 977ff. H. Rombach, 'Erfahrung, Erfahrungswissenschaft', in *Lexikon der Pädagogik*, I (Freiburg, 1970), pp. 375ff. For more detailed discussion of individual problems, cf. J. M. Hinton, *Experiences, An Inquiry into Some Ambiguities* (Oxford, 1973); R. Needham, *Belief, Language and Experience* (Chicago, 1973).

2. H. Rombach, loc. cit.

3. Cf. W. Kasper, 'Tradition als Erkenntnisprinzip, Zur theologischen Relevanz der Geschichte', in *Theol. Quartalschrift*, 155 (1975), pp. 198-215.

4. Cf. K. Sauerland, *Diltheys Erlebnisbegriff, Entstehung, Glanzzeit und Verkümmerung eines literarhistorischen Begriffs* (Berlin & New York, 1972).

5. Cf. P. Ricoeur, 'Le conflit des interprétations', in *Essais d'herméneutique* (Paris, 1969); cf. also the contribution by R. Schreiter in this issue.

6. Cf. D. Mieth, 'Der Wissenschaftscharakter der Theologie', in *Freiburger Zeitschrift für Philosophie und Theologie*, 23 (1976), pp. 13-41, esp. p. 30ff.

7. Cf., J. Mouroux, *L'Expérience chrétienne, Introduction à une théologie* (Paris, 1952), p. 24.

8. Cf. B. Schüller, 'Die Bedeutung der Erfahung für die Rechtfertigung sittlicher Verhaltensregeln', in K. Demmer, B. Schüller, eds., *Christlich glauben und handeln* (Düsseldorf, 1977), pp. 261-86.

9. Cf. the historico-scientific studies by H. Rombach, *Substanz, System, Struktur*, 2 vols. (Freiburg, 1965-66).

10. Cf. finally: K. Rahner, *Grundkurs des Glaubens* (Freiburg, 1976), pp. 31f.

11. Cf. H. M. Baumgartner, *Kontinuität und Geschichte, Zur Kritik und Metakritik der historischen Vernunft* (Frankfurt, 1972).

12. Cf. D. Mieth, op. cit., pp. 24ff.

13. Cf. Kessler, Schöpf, Wild, 'Erfahrung', op. cit., p. 385: 'Experience proves to be such a difficult concept to grasp philosophically, because on the one hand it contradicts theology while at the same time being so closely linked to it, the result being that it can only escape from its clutches by turning theology against itself'.

14. Cf. D. Mieth, 'Die Bedeutung der menschlichen Lebenserfahrung', in *Concilium* 12 (1976), pp. 623-33 (not in English).

15. D. Sölle, *Die Hinreise* (Stuttgart, 1975), p. 43.

16. J. B. Metz, *Followers of Christ* (London & New York, 1978), pp. 7ff.

17. E. Fromm, *To Have or To Be?* (New York & London, 1976).

18. Sölle, op. cit., p. 44.

# PART III

*Revelation and Experience in Regard to Language and Society*

Robert Schreiter

# The Specification of Experience and the Language of Revelation

A STUDY of the interaction between experience and revelation leads one to explore three distinct but interconnected concerns. The first of these is the specification or encoding of experience. In other words, how is experience moulded into some communicable form that allows it to be more publicly available and capable of being shared by a community? Such a specification or encoding also allows one to return to the experience again and again.

A second concern is how such encoded experience achieves the status of revelation in a community. What is the process by which a community perceives that what it has experienced is not reducible to the community itself, but represents a communicative activity encompassing the community and God? The encoded experience then has a privileged status within the community and becomes foundational for the community's sense of identity.

The third concern has to do with revelation itself as a source for new experience. Revelation, the result of communicative interaction between God and the community, becomes itself a pole in further communicative activity as the community specifies new experience. These new interactions may in a variety of ways alter or reencode the revelation.

One common element which binds these concerns together is *language*. Language serves as perhaps the most common medium for encoding experience, although art, ritual and drama do so as well. Language is certainly the most publicly available and easy to share encoding of a community's experience. The Scriptures have served classically as the primary locus of that experience of the people of God which has come to be known as revelation; and the study of revelation often amounts to a study of the language or text of the Scriptures. And finally, in the encounter between experience and revelation, it is primarily in their language that both experience and revelation undergo the most notable change. Creativity in this area will be marked by linguistic innovation. One way, then, to explore the three concerns noted above is to study the rôle of language in the process.

Now the study of language, and especially religious language, has been subjected to many vicissitudes in the past fifty years. In order to locate which approaches to the study of language will be most helpful in our search, it would be good to survey first some of the paths that have been taken in the past fifty years.

## SHIFTS IN THE STUDY OF RELIGIOUS LANGUAGE

There have been three major approaches to the study of language, and especially religious language, which deserve our attention here. In the first approach, religious language was studied to ascertain the quality of religious knowledge and the linguistic status of theological propositions. The main purpose was to ferret out any illegitimate uses of language in religious discourse, where nonsense was masking as propositions about the empirical world. The criterion used for this was empirical verifiability—whether the statement had a referent in the empirical world. Language not passing muster on this account was consigned to the dustbin of 'emotive' language; that is, language which simply provided an outlet for inchoate emotions.[1]

This approach proved to be far too narrow. Many meaningful propositions (including some from philosophers advocating this approach to religious language) could not meet these requirements. This approach was concerned with a genuine knowledge of the world; but the world proved to be too complex for such a simple method. Moreover, most of religious language fell outside the pale of empirical verifiability. While this may have pleased some opponents of religious language, it could not account for the widespread occurrence of religious discourse.

The cul-de-sac of the first approach prompted a second kind of attempt. Researchers began to reflect on the variety of ways in which language was used, and concentrated their efforts on trying to identify these various ways. Whereas 'empirical' had been the watchword in the first approach, 'use' became the rallying point in the second. Within the realm of religious language, all sorts of different uses came to be identified: confessional, performative, disclosive, evocative, and so on.[2]

This approach did show a great deal of sensitivity to the range of religious language, but it continued to run into two problems. Firstly, no overarching method controlled the proliferation of various 'uses' discovered—the catalogues of uses offended a sense of scientific parsimony. And secondly, the 'uses' were constantly raising questions about *meaning* and about larger, metaphysical problems about the relation of language to life. These questions bared the narrow functionalist approach to the meaning of language as its use.

A third approach has tried to meet some of these problems. It seems language as an encoded sign-system which, interwoven with other sign-systems (behaviour patterns, social and economic relations) becomes a network of communication which we call 'culture'. Whereas the first approach was concerned with empirical knowledge, and the second with the function and use of language, this approach lays emphasis on language as a network of communication, involved in a connectedness with other sign-systems as expressive forms of culture.[3] Rather than use, this approach concentrates upon *meaning* and linguistic innovation as a way of binding together the various aspects of experience and culture. Religious language, then, is seen as a framework or system-builder which draws together a variety of other sign-systems in the culture, and thereby communicates values foundational to a society throughout the network of culture.

One particular element in religious language which has received a good deal of attention in this process of communication is *metaphor*. Although originally a concern of poetics and rhetoric, studies have been done on the religious use of metaphor,[4] its functions in philosophical discourse,[5] and within the framework of symbolic anthropology.[6] Metaphor can be defined here as the predication of one sign-image, with its semantic domain, upon another semantic domain. In what follows, we will investigate how the metaphor serves as a catalyzing agent in the interaction of experience and revelation. First of all, we will explore how the metaphor brings about a specification or encoding of experience; then, how it develops a framework which we will call the language of faith; and finally, how it contributes to linguistic creativity as an index of the mutual expansion of experience and revelation. To illustrate this process, we will use examples from the gradual specification of the experience of Jesus as the revelation of God in the NT and succeeding period.

## METAPHOR AND THE SPECIFICATION OF EXPERIENCE

Experience comes to us in an inchoate fashion, as that 'blooming, buzzing reality' (William James) which calls for definition. The encounter with inchoate experience prompts two sets of questions within the subject. On the one hand, the inchoate experience raises questions about the world from which this experience came: where is its place of origin and how is it to be reconciled with the world as it has been known? On the other hand, it raises questions about the receiving subject: his relation to that world, to his previous experiences and to the frameworks at his disposal for coming to terms with that experience within his own sense of subjectivity.

In other words, the encounter with inchoate experience calls for some *specification* of that experience. The process of that specification shapes the identity of the subject and his relation to the world. The process of achieving identity is a matter of giving adequate form to the experience so that it becomes more publicly available, which will allow it to be placed in perspective and communicated to others. Likewise, the process involves connecting that shaped experience with other domains of human life, to allow it to become a shared experience and take its place within the total fabric of the community's life.

This specification of experience, then, involves rescuing it from its inchoate character. This is generally achieved by bringing it into contact with the classification systems of a culture which encode an unknown, inchoate reality into a more known, better formed part of a larger picture of social life. These classification systems carry the intellectual and affective freight of an experience. The fit between the experience and the classification system will be more or less adequate, depending upon the nature of the experience and the complexity of the classification system.[7]

One of the most common ways for specifying experience and encoding it into a classification system is via the predication of a metaphor. Metaphoric predication—by means of which a known, semantic domain is said to be equivalent with the inchoate, unknown semantic domain of the experience—is achieved by an intuitive leap. The sudden bringing together of these two domains prompts a series of activities which set the process of achieving meaning into motion. The freshness of the leap provides the first possibility of perspective, by allowing the subject to disengage himself from the experience and start coming to terms with it. In predication, the metaphor brings to the inchoate experience a domain which has at once a known focus and a larger, uncharted semantic field within which to map out the intellectual and affective terrain of the experience. The known focus provides a touchstone for making the connection between the experience and the larger domain. The uncharted aspects of the semantic field allow new dimensions in the experience to emerge, which had been previously obscured by the inchoate movements within the experience.

An example of this process of the specification of experience can be found in the NT. The experiences which the disciples of Jesus had after his death were inchoate and unprecedented in nature. Much of early NT history can be read as an account of the gradual specification of these experiences by multiple metaphoric predications. One of the first steps was to identify these experiences with Jesus of Nazareth. The Emmaus story (Lk 24:13-35) and Magdalene's mistaking Jesus for the gardener (Jn 20:10-18) reflect this process of specification. Jesus provided a known focus within the predication process. But at the same time the complexity of his life and ministry offered a semantic field within which to bring about further specification. For example, one way of relating to the earthly Jesus was that he was a prophet sent from God. Since part of the semantic field of Jesus was that he was perceived as a prophet, the visions and pneumatic experiences of Jesus could be specified as a prophetic call to the disciples to continue the mission and teaching of Jesus. Thus, they too were called to the ministry of prophecy and preaching. The memory of Jesus could form a focus, while the implications of that historical memory led to a further specification of the experience.

The more compelling the experience, the more likely that there will be a process of multiple predication. With Jesus, the process of specifying the pneumatic experiences continued. A variety of metaphors were employed to specify even further the experience of Jesus. 'Son', 'Christ', 'Son of Man', 'Son of David', 'Lord', and so on, were predicated, drawing upon semantic domains available in the Palestinian environment. Each of these predications brought with it a known focus and a wider semantic field which helped specify the experience of Jesus. Certain elements within each of these semantic fields would be used; others would be rejected. For example, some sapiential aspects of the title 'Son of David' would be predicated of Jesus; while other, davidic-dynastic aspects of the title would not.[8] Particularly through multiple predication does it become possible to ratify and extend a classification system so that it can provide for the future specification of any experience purported to be of Jesus. Thus the NT could be called a record of a predication process for specifying the experience of Jesus.

### THE METAPHORIC FRAMEWORK AS THE LANGUAGE OF FAITH

Heretofore we have dwelt upon the first set of questions about an inchoate experience: namely, those about the world and how the classification systems of a culture give it specificity. But questions are raised about the receiving subject as well. The movement between the known focus and the relatively uncharted semantic field result in a concomitant movement in the subject. The movement between focus and semantic field is generally not only a matter of specifying experience along known paths, but of permitting innovative aspects of the experience to arise. These innovative aspects may either exploit those uncharted areas of the semantic field, or they may call into question the adequacy of the metaphoric bond and change the original, predicated domain. In this latter case, the conclusion is reached that the experience had been less than adequately focussed by the metaphoric predication. This process we see also in the NT. An example would be the title 'Son' which comes to take on meanings beyond the meanings first connected with it (that is, as a special messenger from God); one sees this in the emergence of 'Son' as a Trinitarian predication, to the extent where, by the time of Nicaea, it has lost the subordinationist aspects of the original semantic field.[9]

When the metaphoric bond has been found to be adequate, the affective movement within the subject is directed toward acknowledgment of the adequacy of the bond and is led to an act of confession. In the latter case, the adjusted focus also leads to confession, once the adjustment has been completed.

This process, ending in confession, brings about an important shift in the rôle of the classification system. The classification system, with its sets of metaphoric predications, no longer serves as an ad hoc specification of experience. Rather, it becomes a grid[10] that serves for the specification of any further experience. While one can expand upon and within semantic fields, the metaphoric predications, and their (corrected) foci, become basically standard for any future specification of experience. As a foundational grid for the identity of the subject and the community, they achieve the status of revelation, as extending in its categories beyond the sum total of the community's experiences to be in touch with deeper, constitutive realities. The NT can be seen as such a revelatory grid.

With this status, the grid serves not only as a template for inchoate experience, but directs the specified experience into a communication of particular values. Certainly one of the central values which the NT grid of Jesus as Son came to communicate was the sonship of all men, and finally, Jesus' unique relation to God and God's full revelation in Jesus.

Within the grid, once carefully construed metaphor can become *symbols* which serve as rallying points for the community. This is one important difference between ad hoc classification systems and revelatory grids. One great example of this within the NT is Paul's development of a theology of the *cross*, where once somewhat improbably metaphors (the sign of death as the sign of salvation and life) become key nodes in Christian identity.

The grid, as a relatively consistent, inwardly coherent classification system of metaphoric predications and symbols thus takes on a life of its own. To use this grid is to be part of a special community. To communicate one's experience by means of this grid is to be within the circle of faith. To accept this grid and its metaphoric bonds as adequate to the experience is to admit its foundational, revelatory character.

## REVELATION AND SEMANTIC INNOVATION

But while certain experiences help co-form certain classification systems which in turn become grids, the process does not end here. That dialectic between subject and experience continues. The semantic fields within the grids continue to unfold in new and different ways by the variety of subjects and experiences. The metonymic expansion of the semantic fields in the grid can, in turn, cause some shifts or revisions in the known focus of the metaphoric bond. In Christian history for example, such was the case with the predications made at the first ecumenical Councils, which can be read as intending to correct the foci and so set down certain negative boundaries around the semantic fields. In the great predications 'Jesus is truly God' and 'God has become man', the relations between the domains in the metaphoric bond had to be adjusted. Thus the need for the negative formulation of Chalcedon 'asugchutos, atreptos, adiaretos, achoristos' (DS 302) to specify the focus of the bond, while leaving the semantic fields unexplored. As a result of this, constant contact with the grid itself can become the source of semantic innovation, of new experience and meaning. One sees this in the continuing discussion on the two natures in the immediate post-Chalcedonian period.

The revelatory grid not only aids in the specification of experience for a community, but binds the community together in another communicative activity: ritual. While we cannot go into detail here, ritual, with its episodic structure, allows for regional expansion of a semantic field; in its hymns of praise suggests new forms of multiple predication (litanies); and because of the dramatic and episodic structure, allows one to progress back through the various predications to the 'original experience' as the moment of birth of the revelatory experience itself.[11] Perhaps it is for this reason that the *lex orandi* has always figured so strongly in the specification of experience in the Christian tradition. For generally speaking, semantic innovations occurring within worship have always been of decisive importance for Christians throughout the ages.

What are some of the implications of understanding revelation and experience's interaction as a metaphoric process?

In the first place, it can give a more adequate account of the notion of the development of doctrine and the unfolding of revelation. Rather than trying to deal with the development of doctrine in terms of the translation of discrete intellectual systems (as in the shift from the semitic Logos to the Hellenistic Logos in the development of the notion of the Son), it can be seen as metonymic expansion of a semantic field within a metaphoric predication which leads to a series of shifts in the focus of the metaphoric bond. This seems to account better for the affective movement of revelation, and the sorts of innovation which take place that cannot be accounted for intellectually.

Secondly, it can clarify the rôle of the community and its activity upon the development (and closure) of revelation. The community explores a variety of semantic fields within the various dimensions of multiple predication and so comes to set up boundaries (as at Chalcedon) within which the specification of experience has to fall. Gradually these boundaries come to coalesce into a more or less firm grid.

Third, seeing the metaphoric predication in terms of focus and semantic field allows us to see both the specificity and the indeterminate character of a body of revelation. While the framework for examining experience is fairly well delineated, much of the content demands an encounter with a variety of subjects and new inchoate experiences to be actualized.

In sum then, metaphor allows the various dimensions of the interaction of experience and revelation to emerge, seen as a communicative activity in expressive culture. The impact of experience and subject upon the focus and semantic field in the metaphoric bond could provide the beginnings of a new paradigm for understanding the role of revelation as constitutive of a community.

## Notes

1. The classic text here is A. J. Ayer, *Language, Truth and Logic* (London, 1936).

2. A good example of this approach is F. Ferré, *Language, Logic and God* (New York, 1961).

3. Broadly speaking, this is known as the semiotic study of language. Cf. e.g., U. Eco, *A Theory of Semiotics* (Bloomington, Ind., 1975).

4. S. Teselle, *Speaking in Parables: A Study in Metaphor and Theology* (Philadelphia, 1975).

5. P. Ricoeur, *La Métaphore vive* (Paris, 1975); id., 'The Metaphorical Process', in *Semeia,* 5 (1975), pp. 75-106.

6. R. Wagner, *Habu. Innovation in Daribi Religion* (Chicago, 1972); G. Reichel-Dolmatoff, *Amazonian Cosmos* (Chicago, 1971); J. Fernandez (The Mission of Metaphor in Expressive Culture', in *Current Anthropology,* 15 (1974), pp. 119-45.

7. For an approach to classification systems, cf. C. Levi-Strauss *La Pensée Sauvage* (Paris, 1962).

8. Cf. E. Schillebeeckx, *Jezus het Verhaal van een Levende* (Bloemendaal, 1974), pp. 367-74.

9. For the prehistory of this movement, cf. M. Hengel, *Der-Sohn Gottes* (Tübingen, second ed., 1976).

10. I take the concept 'grid' here from Mary Douglas, *Natural Symbols* (London, second ed., 1973) who defines it as an articulated, shared system of classification.

11. Fernandez, op. cit., pp. 124-29, takes this matter up in more detail.

Bernard Plongeron

# The Languages of Tradition and Social Models

IN THE PERSPECTIVE of a history of religious attitudes, or mentalities in the sense of modern French religious historiography, to say that revelation moulded the Christian West is far too inadequate and vague a statement of the matter. Societies are never content to receive revelation passively. Far from showing the apparent docility of Moses in Sinai, they have always interpreted and proclaimed revelation through their particular, collective images of anguish and hope. Furthermore, the 'Christian West' is an extremely abstract notion, for the epithet 'Christian' has been and can be applied to very different forms of western society which see revelation accordingly.

The relationship between the mode or agent of revelation and that which is revealed becomes very complex when societies, instead of being faultless vehicles of revelation itself, in fact aim at self-revelation for their own sake, by means of the Christian revelation they acclaim as their own. That precisely is the function of tradition or traditions (both apostolic and ecclesiastical) which convey an experience of faith and are located historically in space and time.

Theologians can no longer ignore the fact that tradition—however one defines it—poses three kinds of social questions in its own regard:

(a) socio-cultural: if it is true to say that tradition as the living expression of revelation is the oral or written transmission of the words and works of one generation to another;
(b) *political,* inasmuch as they engage in social practice: 'do this in memory of me . . .'. This demands a liturgy and a dogmatic orthodoxy, which in their turn require an authority: who and what guarantee the secular transmission of the message? This

dual problem is resolved by the organization of faculties; already we have, by means of ecclesiology, two opposing kinds of society: the Reformation world favouring a Church without such powers, and the Counter-Reformation world acknowledging only a Church with unique powers;

(c) *ideological,* since it is a question of knowing in the complex of Church-and-society what revelation is, every statute of that knowledge, above all of a religious kind, is rooted in a certain understanding of the world which is not only idealistic but intends some effect on the actual societies of this world. Whether by force of arms or missions, this world-view seeks to obtain the political and economic means that will enable it to dominate those societies.

Combinations of these three kinds of problems give rise to the various readings of revelation by means of which western societies have presented and justified themselves for two thousand years. This can be adequately illustrated by a few relevant examples: the transitions in the fifth century from the *indiscreta societas* to western 'Christianity'; the Christian 'supervision' in the world of the Counter-Reformation which sacralized writing; the return to 'living reality' in those societies which discovered the thrust of existence at the end of the nineteenth and at the beginning of the twentieth centuries.

## FROM THE 'HARMONY' OF THE SOCIETAS INDISCRETA TO THE 'HIERARCHY' OF WESTERN CHRISTIANITY (FIFTH CENTURY)

Ireneaus, who had been translated from Asia to the see of Lyons in the second century offered a universalist conception when, in his *Adversus Haereses,* he stated: 'In order to understand Scripture one must resort to the Church, and allow oneself to be trained in its bosom and nurtured on the holy Scriptures' (V, 20, 2). The Church of Irenaeus had the features of a world that had not yet dissociated East from West, that of the *Pax romana* and its ability to assimilate languages, institutions and customs of the nations of Europe and Asia, as far as the point of cancelling space and time. Hence that easy manipulation of Christian tradition which excluded any imperialist notions, and any national rivalry, which Irenaeus expressed in a splendid piece of writing:

It is this proclamation (kerygma) which the Church received (from the apostles). It is this faith which constitutes its tradition. Although it is dispersed all over the world, the Church retains that faith as carefully as if it inhabited a single house, and it keeps faith with it as unanimously as if it had only one soul and one heart. With perfect uniformity it preaches it, teaches it and hands it on as if it had but one tongue. Of course languages differ, but the strength of tradition is one and the same. The churches established in the Germanic lands have but one faith, and no other tradition. The same is true of the churches established among the Iberians, the Celts, and in the East, in Egypt, in Libya, and at the centre of the world. (III, 24, 1)

This was a unanimity founded on the basis of an undivided society, on the flexibility of interchange between communities which exchanged letters and brothers, on the flexibility too of a hierarchy in which Rome was only 'chief in love', as Ignatius of Antioch writes to his beloved Ephesians: 'I do not give you orders, as if I were an individual . . . Your venerable presbytery, truly worthy of the Lord, is united with the bishop as the chords of a lyre with the lyre itself'. It is not by chance that this second bishop of Antioch who was condemned to the arena under Trajan, was the first to call all Christians the 'Catholic' Church.

It was a universal society in which the laity were allowed to teach, which enabled Jerome to recommend priests 'not to blush when they learn something from informed laymen about their priestly office, and to spend their days and nights in studying the Scriptures rather than in constructing arguments on the basis of hypotheses . . .' This society believed in life exhibited in the practice of liturgy (catechesis and the eucharist), rather than in speculation and the exercise of faculties.

It was a society of 'perfect agreement' and of 'harmony'—the watchwords of the Fathers of the first four centuries, which were recalled by Pope Leo in the fifth century when he addressed the people of Rome: 'In the unity of faith and of baptism, we make up a homogeneous assembly (*indiscreta societas*), and we participate in a common dignity . . .'[1]

That was no longer wholly true, for at that time Leo was facing the hordes of Attila. He was the effective symbol of a *Pax romana* which had shattered under the barbarian invasions, and of the collapse of the West (Rome was taken in 476) henceforth separated from the East in matters that no form of ecumenism would ever really reconcile, and of the end of a world weighed down by barbarian cultures and institutions, among which the Church remained the ultimate fixed point.

In the convulsions of the fifth century from which medieval Christianity was eventually to emerge, the mentalities of the Christian West followed two apparently contradictory lines of development: a feeling or a sense of political power linked to cultural power, and fear and panic brought about by social chaos and human and material insecurity.

It was at the point of admixture of these two courses of development that a certain 'crystallization' of tradition took place which has lastingly affected the western spirit.

The Church-society came under the spell of what today we call power and civilization. It did not ask for this, but in the universal cataclysm it remained the only stable political organization, the rampart of civilization behind its monastic citadels in which manuscripts, art, science and technical achievement found refuge: Lérins, Ireland, Monte Cassino, and so on.

Forced to take over the political hegemony, the papacy broke with the 'harmony' of the other major communities. At Chalcedon (451), which debated the dogma of the Incarnation, Leo of Rome imposed his authority, to the acclamations of the Fathers who caused the following to be written to Bossuet: 'Peter has spoken through the lips of Leo'.[2] Previously Leo had rejected the canon of Ephesus (431) in accordance with which the see of Constantinople was to have been elevated above all the eastern sees. Leo rejected this decision 'by virtue of the authority of the apostle Peter', which shows a sense of tradition which hardly fits easily with that of the *indiscreta societas* and which foretells however faintly the famous claim of Boniface VIII regarding the 'submission of all human beings to the Roman pontiff' in the bull *Unam Sanctam* (1302).

Already social relations, henceforth understood as relations of compulsion, changed from dominant to dominated: from being 'horizontal' lines between the communities of the *indiscreta societas*, they tended to become 'verticals' in the process of Roman centralization, and the birth of an authoritarian, clerical civilization that was soon established on the basis of monastic feudalism: the earth and the men of the earth.

The transmission of tradition became calcified in its turn and, instead of going 'hand in hand' as in the first few centuries, it came to have in a quasi-superstitious relation to Scripture, which is a sign of power in oral societies. At the beginning of the fifth century, Jerome sealed the Roman canonical Scriptures with the Vulgate, henceforth to be the common 'norm' of the Christian West. As for the interpretation of this norm, Vincent of Lérins put forward the following golden rule in the first half of the century: 'In the Catholic Church itself, we have carefully to ensure that we keep to what has always been believed everywhere and by everyone . . .' This *quod ubique, quod ab omnibus* of the *Commitorium* was to delight the 'grammatologists' of the seventeenth century in twenty-five editions for Europe and twelve translations for France alone.

We have to try to grasp the ideology of this new form of western Christianity. At the end of the century, the Pseudo-Denys the Areopagite produced his *De ecclesiastica hierarchia,* by introducing, as he did, the term 'hierarchy' into the ecclesiastical vocabulary.[3] It was no accident that the Middle Ages christened the Pseudo-Denys the *Doctor hierarchicus* who stated that because God was its founder, the ecclesiastic hierarchy could suffer no harm; hence it was a hierarchy of perfection in which no superior was accountable to his inferiors.

On the other hand, it is not difficult to sense the uneasy aspect of this socio-religious interpretation of authority sacralizing Scriptures, and *vice versa.* It is not so much a will to power that was the main concern but the organization of social chaos in a western world ravished by the barbarians. It was a chaos with a taste for death and one against which Augustine fought desperately. He offered his *City of God* as a political theology of the West, at a time when everything was about to collapse. As the historian Lucien Febvre has shown,[4] these barbarian times not only weakened man but made him a dangerous entity for his fellow beings. There was a brutality of behaviour no longer held in check by vanished institutions, and a brutality of nature which could no longer be dominated because of the lack of technical aids. Driven to the point of sheer existence, men kept to what had already been handed down. There was a decay of learning and a fear of new things.

Elementary prudence demanded repetition, which was the function of the earliest medieval thinkers: their form of security consisted in scrupulous commentaries on the *auctoritates,* which were Aristotle and the Bible. The Christian West was so marked by this that it once again took refuge in mere repetition: St Thomas and the scholastic *lectio;* Gothic art and its flamboyant form of repetition embellishing the original.

The cleric's task is to serve tradition and at the same time to comment on it indefinitely. The rise of the Talmudic commentaries with Rachi, the 'prince of commentators' and the greatest Jewish educator of the eleventh century, shows clearly that it is an experience of universal society and not of a crisis inherent in Christian tradition. The imagery is very revealing: the ornamental letter, the illuminated Bible or haggadah of the thirteenth to the fourteenth centuries[5] offend against this desire to achieve duration through Scripture and a life set in the framework of what already is. Too great insistence on the oral character of these medieval societies betokens neglect of the superstitious cultivation of Scripture by repeating it, an inheritance which extended to the classical age (the 'culture' of Molière's doctors) and which was not without influence on the interpretation of tradition in the Reformation period.

## 'SUPERVISION' AND GRAMMATOLOGY IN CHRISTIANITY IN THE CLASSICAL AGE (SIXTEENTH TO EIGHTEENTH CENTURIES)

Theologians and historians still argue about the distinction made between Scripture and tradition by the 1546 decree of the Council of Trent. First, one should note, at the level of religious attitudes, the interest of this factual dualism, for the decree speaks of the Christian truth in 'libris scriptis et sine scripto traditionibus'—in written books *and* in non-written traditions; and it is very careful not to confuse 'sine scripto' with 'the oral'. The ambiguity of the formula allows interpretations of 'and' which join or separate Scripture and 'tradition', according to the types of society to which the commentators belong.

But everyone agrees on the way in which the decree twice defines revelation: 'source of all saving truth and of all moral laws'. What is the original expression for 'moral law'? In both cases, the text speaks of *disciplina,* which amounts to *veritas.* We think, of course, of the theology of Augustine, for whom, at the end of his life *disciplina* was a basic idea, especially in his arguments against the Donatists. Augustine understood it as a coercive and magisterial power of the Church, but he allowed this religious constraint a certain dynamic virtue: *disciplina* moves from an outward state undergone by the Christian to an 'inward' form of reception. It is the educational means of understanding the faith. But this pedagogical method is not without political sanction, for Augustine takes the word *disciplina* from the usage of the Roman administration: the *administrator disciplinae* is the official charged with respect for the law.[6] It would seem above all to have been this political and 'supervisory' office that was retained by the Tridentine Fathers when they defined the Christian orthodoxy of the modern era with these two words: 'fides et mores'. Henceforth all experience of faith would be authenticated in terms of 'faith and morals'. Obviously we have then to know what 'morals' are, and whether they inform faith, or the other way round.

Two recent studies[7] shows that the conciliar acts do not offer any explanation in themselves of the introduction and recommended application of this norm of 'faith and morals'. The scholastic commentaries would seem to show that *mores* indicates a notion of morals founded on revelation, which takes us back to Augustinian theology.

The history of religious attitudes suggests a much more political explanation. *Disciplina,* with 'fides et mores' as its criterion, intends a moralization of society by means of religion. Its full meaning in the France of the eighteenth century is consistent with the use of *police* which, as the dictionaries of the period show, means 'in its most general sense, laws, order and conduct which are to be observed for the sustaining and continuance of states and societies'. As emphasized by the *Dictionnaire de Police* by La Poix de Fréminville (1756), the first duty of the royal official concerned with 'this aspect of justice . . . [is] to maintain religion, to ensure that commerce flourishes, and to enrich the subjects of the king . . . the execution of regulations in order to look after public interests, in order to support those of the Church, the king and his lord . . .' *Police* also has a cultural connotation and is the opposite of 'barbarism': 'the savages of America were ignorant of the *maintenance of law and order* and of laws when they were discovered', the italicized words represent the use of the French word 'police', rendered here for convenience as 'supervision'.

The language of the Council of Trent therefore serves this double concept of politico-religious power and culture as a principle of social order. After medieval Christianity, it was the ideological foundation of the western societies which comprised what is known as 'Christian civilization'. In these societies a fundamental norm was imposed on everyone: 'the written, canonical and centralizing law whose guardian is the Church, which was then poured into the social mould of the age: monarchical, pyramidal and "hierarchological" ' (Congar).

This was the result of an understanding of revelation controlled only by the teaching Church, as Bellarmine put it: 'Scripture is a rule of faith, and not a total but a partial rule. The total rule of faith is the word of God or *the revelation which God has given to the Church*'. This approximation of revelation to the Catholic Church is extremely useful in constructing a political theology of the *Ancien Régime*. It amounts to the following: the conception of dogma (the religious norm, *fides*) is conditioned by the conception of law (the civil norm, *mores*), and the whole comprises the *disciplina* or 'supervision' which holds sway over society as a whole. Any infraction of this code of socio-religious moralization serves to characterize the 'heretic'.

Heresy before all else was the Reformation, which is quite understandable if we think of Luther's idea of the law. He made *Gewalt* (simultaneously power and authority, force and violence) an absolute beyond any qualification as to its origin or whether the prince is 'just' or 'unjust'. Whereas the Council of Trent firmly united the spiritual and temporal by stressing the *disciplina* which guarantees *veritas*, Luther makes no distinction; he separates the two domains and demands that in the order of absolute supervision by law and order, 'there is no Gospel, conscience, grace . . . and nothing of Christ himself' (*Opera*, XV, p. 129). This brought Marx's comment: 'Luther cancelled belief in authority by restoring the authority of belief',[8] and the authority of belief had already become a democratic option in the social contract.

Beyond, or apart from, these theological debates, the language of tradition, according to the Council of Trent, is that of a Counter-Reformation: that is to say, it is the language of social and political testimony to a model of a society which is to be maintained and imposed on 'heretics'. Yet Catholics belonging to another cultural tradition had reservations about this imperialism of the Latin 'grammatologists'. W. Bishop (1554-1624), apostolic administrator of the Catholics of England, Wales and Scotland, went so far as to express censure on behalf of the attitude of his countrymen living under common law, in accordance with which common sense was also characteristic of the *sensus fidelium*. He asked why there should be this contempt for non-written usage, which 'both the Old Testament and the written law found admissible'. In his *Reformation of a Catholic Deformed,* he defended against the Roman legalists the importance of the oral aspect of the three kinds of tradition: divine, apostolic and ecclesiastical, 'for neither ink, nor paper have conferred any new sacredness, force and value on the words of God and the apostles; uttered orally they have the same value and even credibility as when written down'.

English 'pragmatism' was opposed to the 'hierarchology' which inspired the Counter-Reformation and which was to reach its culmination at Vatican I. As much as and even more than the dogmatic arguments invoked in its favour, pontifical infallibility seemed something of a provocation to societies in the process of freeing themselves from reasons of state, and holding authority maintained for reasons of Church to be inimical when so many believers were calling for a return to 'living religion'. The Modernist crisis was not far distant.

A LOGIC OF LIVED RELIGION. THE NINETEENTH
AND TWENTIETH CENTURIES

The period 1850-1950 was that of the rise of biology, the discovery of real life and its political and philosophical implications, by way of evolutionist and vitalist ideas, the birth of the racial theory which characterized the new philosophies of history, and the establishment of anthropology as an autonomous science around 1860. Continual recourse to a biological vocabulary and metaphors became almost a literary leit-motif of the most varied speculative ideas, and the sign of a transformation of western collective mentalities. Their watchword was 'evolution'.

All dictionary definitions amount to the same thing: 'slow and gradual change'. That was the scientific credo of one of the masters of evolutionary thought, Herbert Spencer (1820-1903), who wished to bridge the gulf between the natural sciences and the human sciences, and avoided any notion of discontinuity. That does not mean that human societies can be directly approximated to animal societies. In his *Principles of Sociology* (three vols., 1877-96), Spencer declared on the contrary that the cells of the biological entity were subordinate to the whole, whereas society should exist for the interest and freedom of each of its members. As against socialism, which he called military despotism, Spencer ratified the socio-political transformation of Europe at the end of the nineteenth century: the birth of the bourgeois democracies on the ruins of monarchical régimes. But before the general collapse of the latter, evolutionists, anthropologists, philologists and manic racists reached agreement in demonstrating that the supremacy of the white race or 'Christian civilization' was an irrefragable aspect of evolution. In spite of the present attitude to his narrow and aggressive nationalism, a large number agreed with Gustav Klemm (1802-1867) that the Germans had given evidence of their moral and intellectual superiority, and that it was to them above all 'that Providence would seem to have entrusted the work of looking after the progress of the human species, for after all German monarchs occupy all the Christian thrones of Europe'.[9] This attitude gave rise to an exaggerated Eurocentrism which had some effect on the religious attitudes of the time.

On this cultural and political basis, Bergsonism is merely a more typical example of the essential trend and deserves consideration as a philosophical experience of faith at a time when Teilhard de Chardin threatens to eclipse one of his inspired predecessors. Bergson's path extended from the *Essay on the Immediate Data of Consciousness* (1889) which was still strongly redolent of Spencer's evolutionism, to the *Two Sources of Morals and Religion* (1932). *Creative Evolution* came in the first third of the journey, in 1907, when Modernism was in full swing.

The first word to strike one in the title of this famous work is the term 'evolution'. One thinks of it as fitting the etymology: 'the action of emerging by unfolding' which recalls the image of a seed from which a plant or an animal unfolds. This recalls, in the order of Christian revelation, the same idea of development which helped the success of Newman's *A Grammar of Assent*.[10] Christian thought took such a long time to assimilate it, that those theologians who opined that the thrust of tradition was to be found in this process from the germ to fruition still seemed startling at Vatican II.

But Bergson's revolutionary idea was the qualification of evolution as 'creative'. A creative evolution reintroduced into change the unforeseen and radical newness of the event: that is, a certain discontinuity. This discontinuity is linked with the creation of existence, or invention.

Especially in *La Pensée et le mouvant* Bergson distinguished 'invention' from 'discovery', those profound ideas which could have transformed a theology of tradition. Such a theology might also have found support in Bergson's theodicy, as presented in its full originality in the third chapter of *Données immédiates,* on the subject of freedom, up to the pages of *Deux Sources* on the God who is perfectly revealed in Jesus Christ.

In the history of religious thought, creation occurs either as a fact of Judeao-Christian revelation, or—in Descartes—as a rational idea. But in both cases it is a divine act. Inasmuch as man is an image of God, he can be called a creator in his own way. Bergsonism is certainly the first metaphysics which produces creators before coming to the existence of a Creator. The act of creation is a fact of consciousness, then a property of life, before it is affirmed in the Love from which life emerges and to which consciousness returns.

This was a daring change in western thought and served to refute the anachronism of the editors of the constitution *Dei Filius* of Vatican I. 'Hierarchology' proved so life-denying that people had come to think that the visible Church, thanks to the magisterium, had become of itself a strong motive for credibility. It proved by itself, so it seemed, that it was the actual mandatory of revelation. One of the most influential conciliar Fathers saw that it was impossible to stay at this Tridentine level of thought. Cardinal Deschamps, the Archbishop of Malines, found some Fènelonesque emphases to describe his colleagues' fixity: 'The testimony of God sought for by human reason is not in any way a dead form of witness but a living word. The divine revelation human reason is looking for is not merely some ancient written monument . . . some book that has to be interpreted laboriously, but a living and fatherly voice to be listened to simply and composed in a manner fit for all rather than one that is laboured and affected'.[11]

Between Pascal, who was an obvious inspiration for Cardinal Deschamps, and Bergson establishing his logic of living existence, Maurice Blondel, with a courage that was nurtured by his Christian belief, discerned in the very thick of the Modernist crisis, the 'vital rôle and philosophic ground of tradition'. That was the title of his article, which appeared first in *La Quinzaine,* with the sub-title 'history and dogma'. The philosopher of *L'Action* wrote in a serious and conscious effort to help his Church to emerge from the state of magisterial sclerosis into which it had fallen: 'Tradition is certainly founded on the texts, but it is grounded at the same time and primarily on something else: on a continuous experience which allows it in certain respects to remain in control of texts instead of being strictly tied down . . . It helps to free us from the Scriptures themselves, to which it nevertheless has continual recourse in a spirit of pious respect (the *pari pietatis affectu* of the 1546 decree); it helps us to reach the real Christ other than by the exclusive route of the texts . . .'

These are probably banal remarks for contemporaries of *Gaudium et Spes* who will find it difficult to discern there a struggle between two types of society. On the one hand, there are the 'Modernists', who would probably be known as 'progressives' nowadays, who believe in the invention power of man as responsible for his destiny as societies are for theirs, yet do not confuse Bergson's *élan vital* with the myth of eternal progress, and reject the hyperrationalism of the German Enlightenment. On the other hand, there are the traditionalists who want government by authority which alone is capable of keeping man in the immaturity he naturally suffered as a result of original sin, and for whom 'evolution', even in the continuous sense, means anarchy. This party found its leader in another major figure of Vatican I, Cardinal Billot. The *De Immutabilitate traditionis* (1907) of the well-known professor at the Gregorian university was a rap across the knuckles of all the 'Modernists' (and Blondel in particular) who, according to Billot, did not view 'tradition other than as a human fact, a form of transmission from generation to generation on the unaided initiative and industry of mankind'.

It would have been enough to have studied Blondel's excellent and still relevant formula, recapitulating Newman and Bergson, to show that the debate between 'immanence' and 'transcendence', now modernized in the form of 'horizontalism' and 'verticalism', was inadequate. Blondel had said clearly: 'Tradition has nothing to innovate, because it possesses its God and its all; but it must continually teach us something new because it transmits something from the implicit lived to the explicit known'.

The fact that the 'unmoving' so beloved of Cardinal Billot should have triumphed (for at least the first quarter of the twentieth century) over the 'logic of lived existence' is only conceivable in the context of a church establishment which can still believe in its political credibility and, in the name of revelation, picture itself as mistress of a 'Christian civilization' with a perfect western narcissism. Even though this illusion shattered on contact with contemporary change, it is no less true that the ecclesial *aggiornamento* still leads as it always leads to a philosophy and therefore a theology of life (contraception, abortion and so on) . . .

## CONCLUSION

This is certainly an argument for some believers today to get rid of the blocks of their Church in order to contact the 'real Christ', as

Blondel said, in an existential experience which rejects tradition conceived as a dead testimony to a dead past.

But that is to forget the lesson of the teachers of *élan vital* who have always been careful to draw attention to the duration in the heart of evolution (cf. Bergson), even though man is an historical being. The historian is aware that the most ardent 'awakenings' and charismatic forms of the act of faith have eventually produced extremely oppressive societies: for instance, the most inquisitorial of all, Calvin's Geneva.

Others, not unromantically, have tried to downgrade tradition by playing at 'early Christians'. I dedicate to these neo-primitivists who think they can recreate Irenaeus' society in our nuclear world the following thought of Bonald's (a master of traditionalist thought, and one who is re-read fervently in Mgr. Lefevre's church): 'Those who have wanted to revive the times of the earliest Christians have always forced political societies towards a state of childhood' *Pensées Diverses*, 1816).

Every personal experience of faith can only increase in quality and depth if it scrutinizes the cultural and political framework in which it occurs, in regard to itself and in regard to the human community in which it occurs. In other words, the history of mentalities on religious attitudes is a revelation of ourselves to ourselves, just as it reveals societies to themselves. The fact that, as Newman says in his *University Sermons*, religion tends to set up institutions and positive laws and is so strong that it takes even temporal laws external to it into its domain, is not to be ascribed simply to historical 'errors'. A 'critical' reading of tradition should assume this ecclesiastical duration, and drop the illusion of a 'naive' reading (in perfect faith, as it were). Otherwise, in order to reach the real Christ, the Christ of faith would be set against the Jesus of history; that would be contrary to the historicism of the last century, but the same rut would threaten.

*Translated by John Griffiths*

## Notes

1. *Sermo* 4; PL, 54, col. 149.
2. *Histoire des Variations des Eglises Protestantes* (1688), bk XIII, ch. 20.
3. A. Faivre, *Naissance d'une Hiérarchie. Les premières étapes du cursus clerical* (Paris, 1977), pp. 172-77.
4. L. Lebvre, *Autour de l'Heptaméron* (Paris, 1944), pp. 228-30.

5. G. G. Scholem, 'Révélation et tradition comme catégories religieuses du Judaïsme', in *Le Messianisme Juif* (Paris, 1974).

6. R. A. Markus, *Saeculum: History and Society in the Theology of St Augustine* (Cambridge, 1970), pp. 75, 142-43.

7. M. Midali, *Rivelazione, Chiesa, scrittura et tradizione all IV sessione del concilio di Trento* (Rome, 1973), esp. ch. 6; T. Lopez Rodriguez, 'Fides et Mores en Trento', in *Scripta Theol. Esp.*, V, 1 (1973), pp. 175-221.

8. M. Simon, *Contribution à la critique de la Philosophie du Droit de Hegel* (Paris, 1971), pp. 81-83.

9. Gustav Klemm, *Allgemeine Kultur. Geschichte der Menschheit* (Leipzig, 1843), vol. IV, p. 232.

10. N. Lash, *Newman on Development. The Search for an Explanation in History* (London, 1975).

11. Quoted by R. Aubert, *Le problème de l'acte de foi* (Leeuven, 1958), p. 195.

# Matthew Lamb

# Dogma, Experience and Political Theology

THE EMERGENCE of church doctrines, or dogmas, is associated with the impact upon Christianity of the logos or conceptuality of Graeco-Roman cultures. Since the Enlightenment, with its critiques of both that conceptuality and Christianity in the name of a new empirical rationality, theologians have faced a dilemma: either dogma or experience. To accept one as normative meant minimizing or rejecting the other as normative. Some theologians opted for the more experiential forms of modern knowledge (for example, Naturalism, Ritschlianism, Liberalism, Modernism); others sought to preserve dogmatic faith either by by-passing the Enlightenment (for example, fundamentalism, fideism), or by insisting upon the validity of the classical conceptuality against the claims of modernity (for example, Protestant neo-orthodoxy, Catholic neo-scholasticism). This article will first briefly sketch a few main criticisms of efforts to solve this dilemma, and then outline a possible response to it in terms of political theology and three different forms of enlightenment.

## DOGMA VERSUS EXPERIENCE?

In spite of many creative theological efforts aimed at adapting traditional dogmas to modern experience (for example, Schleiermacher, Blondel, Chardin, Bultmann, Rahner, Tillich, and the Niebuhrs), serious doubts are still raised about the validity of such mediations. Four criticisms of these efforts are especially relevant to my subject.

Peter Berger's sociology of knowledge, with its appeals to an empirically given 'everyday consciousness' and the minority status of believers in secular society, leads him to insist on the alternatives confronting any theology today. Either one preserves one's religious traditions and confronts modern society critically, or one tries to assimilate those traditions into modernity and thereby risks jeopardizing them. As cognitive minorities in largely secular cultures, Berger sees no way out of this dilemma for contemporary theologies—although, as Berger expresses it, it is probably due as much to his undifferentiated two-kingdom Lutheran theology as to his sociology of knowledge.[1]

Eric Voegelin's philosophical critique of doctrinization is more cogent than Berger's critique of mediation. Voegelin does not oppose dogma to modern experience. Indeed, he sees much of modernity as the social and cultural offspring of 'the general deformation of experiential symbols into doctrines.'[2] The Trinitarian and Christological doctrines of the fourth and fifth centuries were derivative rather than experiential symbols, and conditioned by the theological debates of those times. This doctrinization was deformed into conceptual systems cut off from the true experience of theophanic reality expressed in the narrative or experiential symbols of the New Testament. Such conceptual doctrines, coupled with the hubris of political power, became 'dogmatomachies' in Voegelin's terms: 'This predominance of the doctrinal form has caused the modern phenomenon of the great dogmatomachies, that is of the theological dogmatomachy, and the so-called wars of religion, in the sixteenth and seventeenth centuries A.D., and of the ideological dogmatomachy, and the corresponding revolutionary wars, from the eighteenth to the twentieth centuries A.D.'[3]

Whereas late medieval scholasticism, nominalism, and Cartesianism set the stage for the theological dogmatomachy, it was above all Hegelianism that epitomized an age in revolt against theological and metaphysical dogmatism. Yet Hegel and the post-Hegelians did not recover an experience of reality as theophanic. Instead, they inverted doctrinal language and derailed experience into egophanic ideologies. Greek and biblical narratives, symbolizing the experience of reality as constituted in the tension between divinity and humanity (the *Metaxy*), were degraded into mere projections of an immature self-awareness that is now superseded by 'the egophanic God-man or superman (Feuerbach, Marx, Nietzsche)' who establishes 'the final realm of freedom in history.' These doctrinally derivative God-men or 'Christs' can then 'try to force the Parousia into history in their own person.'[4]

Following a Heideggerian critique of western metaphysics, Bernhard Welte suspects that Nicea, with its emphasis upon *ousia,* represents a conceptually static forgetfulness of being. Such a metaphysics has found its apotheosis in the technocracy of modernity's neo-positivism

and empiricism. If we are to recover the primordial experience of being, then we must criticize the history of western metaphysics and
recognize the limitations of the classical dogmas.[5]

In a similar vein, David Tracy argues for a revisionist approach to
traditional doctrines in the light of criteria adequate to our human
situation and contemporary experience. He finds classical Christian
theism and any exclusivist Christology both inadequate and incoherent
by such criteria.[6] Specifically, he criticizes the political theologies of
praxis—such as those of Moltmann, Metz, Alves, Shaull, Segundo,
Gutierrez, or Soelle—for seeming to ignore this problematic. In Tracy's opinion, these theologians use a transformed neo-orthodox model
which tends to leave the traditional dogmas in their classical forms—as
though their insistence upon orthopraxis covers up their failure to
analyze orthodoxy critically.[7]

Whatever the diversity of perspectives among Berger, Voegelin,
Welte, and Tracy, their various critiques of traditional dogma, when
viewed in the light of their respective positions, agree in three respects:
(1) that any adequate understanding of human experience involves an
intrinsic orientation to the transcendent as sacral; (2) that such an
orientation is more compactly expressed in biblical and other narratives, and may well be lost in doctrinal conceptuality; and (3) that any
reflection on this problematic must, at least negatively, take seriously
the impact of the Enlightenment on modernity.[8]

## THE TRANSFORMATIVE DIMENSION OF POLITICAL THEOLOGY

I call 'political' all those theologies which acknowledge that human
action, or praxis, is not only the goal but the foundation of theory. As I
have indicated elsewhere, such praxis-grounded and praxis-oriented
theologies would include not only the political theology initiated by
Metz, but the theological method articulated by Lonergan, and various
forms of liberation theology.[9] These theologies are not simply neo-
orthodox, if by that one understands a model of theologizing similar to
that of Karl Barth or Hans Urs von Balthasar. For such neo-orthodox
theologies mediate Christian faith by means of supernaturalist
paradoxes; the emphasis is on how revelation so transcends reason that
it in some way negates rational experience. Political theology, on the
other hand, mediates faith dialectically, emphasizing how it transforms
human action.[10] Moreover, where political theologians emphasize the
transformative character of religious truth, Berger, Voegelin, Welte
and Tracy tend to emphasize its disclosive character. All four authors
criticize the dogmatic assumptions of neo-orthodoxy. What they have
not appreciated is the insight of political theology into how neo-

orthodoxy represents the inadequacy of a disclosure model of truth to handle dogma. Although these same authors criticize the tendency of neo-orthodox theologies to minimize the value of empirical and/or historical-critical methods, on the one hand, and phenomenological or ontological reflection, on the other, they formulate their criticisms in terms of the disclosive possibilities of such methods or reflections *vis-à-vis* religious symbols. Where neo-orthodoxy insists upon the disclosive criteria of revelation, our four authors insist upon the necessity of complementing or correlating revelatory symbols with empirical, historical-critical, phenomenological, or ontological disclosive criteria.

The disclosive methods of empirical research, phenomenological hermeneutics, historical-critical analysis, or ontological reflection certainly have contributions to make in theology. They are indispensable or helpful in disclosing the continuous contexts within which theology relates religious traditions to manifold personal, social, and cultural situations of the past and present. Political theology acknowledges this in its concern for interdisciplinary research (Metz), for the methods of the natural and human sciences (Peukert), for the value of the hermeneutical circle (Segundo) and sociological analysis (Baum) to theology, for the disclosive potential of Christian symbols in our contemporary situations (Gutierrez, Metz, Moltmann, Hodgson). In terms of Lonergan's functional specialization, these disclosive methods are especially appropriate to the first phase of theology concerned with an ever more adequate mediation of the past with the present.[11]

But these disclosive methods cannot do full justice either to human experience or to church doctrines. The most such methods can disclose are the dialectically divergent horizons of meaning and value that issue in different results of research, different interpretations, contradictory historical analyses, opposed ontologies, variant societies. It is at this point that neo-orthodoxy raises the banner of religious conversion as the sole criterion capable of disclosing ultimate truth. Humans cannot live from continually revised hypotheses alone. Church dogmatics (Barth) must disclose the true way by confronting human experience with its paradoxical need for religious faith, hope, and love. In criticizing this dogmatic stance, Berger, Tracy, Voegelin and Welte do not regress to liberal scepticism. Instead they seek to articulate (much as Bultmann did *vis-à-vis* Barth) realms of human experience disclosive of transcendence. Through various appeals to limit-experiences (Berger, Tracy) and transcending-experiences (Voegelin, Welte), they seek the ontological foundations from which the doctrinal symbols of the past can be revised (Tracy), or radically relativized (Voegelin).

In the various perspectives of political theology these positions are inadequate in their criticisms of neo-orthodoxy and in their appeals to human experience. A foundational approach to human experience is incomplete or inadequate if it attempts a merely disclosive ontology of limit-experiences or transcending-experiences. For such an approach, no matter how sophisticated, minimizes the transformative effect of religious and doctrinal symbols on human experience. Unlike neo-orthodoxy, political theology attends not only to the transformative import of religious and doctrinal symbols on human experience, but to the transformative structures or dynamics of human experience itself. When limit or transcendence are analyzed phenomenologically or ontologically, their negative and heuristic orientation to the future tends to be overlooked. Limit and transcendence are 'disclosed' as dimensions or structures *already present* implicitly or explicitly in human experience.[12] When they are related to the future or to freedom, the latter are *not* presented as foundational to limit or transcendence but as their consequence or goal.[13] Political theology, however, approaches limit and transcendence as grounded in human praxis, as the latter is negatively constituted by limit and heuristically constituted by transcendence. Limit and transcendence are not disclosed as already present but are experienced as imperative challenges capable of transforming or converting the present unfreedom of human experience. There are many illustrations of this transformative dimension of foundations in political theology. Metz refers to praxis-oriented political theology as foundational theology, and to the way in which ontology masks the future. He and Moltmann elaborate the foundational importance of eschatology (future) and suffering (limit) for theology. Peukert carefully shows how both scientific theory and theology need foundations in a theory of communicative interaction as praxis. Latin American liberation theologians emphasize the actual contexts in which theology is produced. Lonergan sees the foundations of the second phase of functional specialization, concerned with the mediation of the present with the future, as articulating the imperatives of intellectual, moral, and religious conversions. Indeed, Lonergan's intentionality analysis is not so much phenomenologically disclosive as it is praxis-transformative, with its emphasis upon self-appropriation and the levels of conscious activity as imperatives toward transcendence.[14]

The experience of truth in this framework is primarily a transforming correspondence between subject and object, and only if transformation occurs (in either subject or object or both) is there a disclosure of truth. The transformation is praxis, where praxis is understood as conscious performance or doing in contrast both to production or making and to theory or definition. This distinguishes political theology's notion of praxis from materialistic or idealistic uses of the term. While Aristotle's distinction between *praxis* as human conduct or doing and *poiesis* as human production or making is relevant here, political theology reverses the primacy of theory over praxis. Where Aristotle subordinated *praxis* and *poiesis* to disclosive theory, political theology subordinates theory and production to praxis. Where Hegel sublates praxis and production into theory as absolute knowledge, political theology sublates theory and production into praxis as conscious and free performance.[15] Similarly, where Marx tends to sublate theory and praxis into production as materialist infrastructure, political theology sees this as a crypto-positivism in Marx's notion of praxis and insists that production should be sublated by praxis.[16]

This notion of human experience and action as primarily transformative has profound and widespread implications. Theory and definition, as well as production and making, are understood as disclosive consequences of a transformative or self-correcting process of learning.[17] Transformation is foundationally intrinsic to education and enlightenment whereas disclosure is derivative. This marks a radically new understanding of enlightenment inasmuch as attention is directed to the dialectically transformative praxis of enlightenment. This is radically new, not because transformative praxis was not operative in, for instance, the enlightenments associated with the Greek philosophical and medieval theological shifts toward theory, or in the modern Enlightenment with its shift towards empirically technical rationality. It is radically new since those enlightenments tended to control transformative praxis either by theory (classical) or by empirical technique (modern). Political theology is part of a contemporary enlightenment seeking to establish transformative praxis as the control of both theory and empirical technique.[18] For the sake of brevity, I shall sketch the different understandings of church doctrines or dogmas according to enlightenments successively giving priority first to theory, then to empirical technique, and finally to praxis.

### THREE ENLIGHTENMENTS AND DOGMA

1. *A classical theoretical enlightenment* occurred in the medieval reception of Graeco-Roman theory in theology. In the twelfth and thirteenth centuries theology flourished as it incorporated more and more Hellenic and Patristic notions into its commentaries, *Quaestiones*, and *Summae*. If the Aristotelian notion of *episteme* influenced the Schoolmen's ideal of scientific theory, their understanding of wisdom was drawn from Patristic receptions of Middle and Neo-Platonic notions of a hierarchy of being attained pre-eminently through contemplative *theoria*. These provided disclosive paradigms theoretically projecting and reflecting a hierarchical order in the spiritual and material universe, society, and the Church. Theology as a speculative and practical science, subordinate to the vision of God as First Truth,

hierarchically ordered the multiplicity of nature, human conduct, and revealed truths within the framework of a creative *exitus* and redemptive *reditus* to that Truth.[19] Church doctrines were understood as credal formulae or symbols disclosive of the Church's faith in the revelation of the apostolic doctrines contained in sacred Scripture. Biblical narrative and dogma were united in the schema of hierarchically revealed truths of faith. Hence, for Aquinas, the central Trinitarian and Christological mysteries were explicitly believed in by the major figures in pre-Judaic and Old Testament times, although they had to veil those mysteries in figurative language for the less wise (*minores*) people of those times. The superior wisdom of the major figures was due to their hierarchical pre-eminence in the redemptive return of all things to God.[20] The doctrinal symbols, however, were not severed from the transformative experience of conversion in so far as Aquinas, and even more Bonaventure, stressed the negative (*via negatonis, pati divina*) and heuristic (for example, psychological analogy of the Trinity) aspects of participation in the ontological hierarchy.[21]

These negative and heuristic elements were increasingly sundered from experience in the perceptualism and logical pedantry of fourteenth-century scholasticism. If, as Peter Gay contends, 'hierarchy' was the master metaphor of the Middle Ages, decadent scholasticism deformed the metaphysics of the metaphor into logical contradictions (for instance, Ockham's theological fideism legitimated the 'papal tyranny' he politically abhorred). Mysticism retreated from the academic disputes of the schools and, in the fifteenth century, Nicholas of Cusa could attempt to reinstate the hierarchical theophany of the universe only by privatizing it.[22] The subsequent Tridentine scholasticism of Cajetan, Cano, or Suarez solidified a conceptualistic doctrinization (in Voegelin's sense) that severed dogma from experiential symbols. The stage was set for an authoritarian practice of the hierarchical magisterium scarcely attentive to the transformative praxis of the *sensus fidelium*. Catholic manual theology was, in the limit, to become more subaltern to papal pronouncements than to God as First Truth.[23]

2. *A modern technical enlightenment,* from its tentative beginnings in the seventeenth and eighteenth centuries to its maturity in the nineteenth and twentieth centuries, removed the study of history from its tutelage to any metaphor of hierarchy (still so evident in Counter-Reformation writings) and gradually established the empirical criteria of historical-critical methods. Just as the empirical methods of the natural sciences replaced the primacy of classical theory, so the development of new empirical techniques replaced an interest in any divine hierarchical ordering of history (the *exitus-reditus* theme) with

an interest in history as *made* or *produced* by men. Ranke's famous 'how it actually happened' was not guided by a disclosive metaphor of hierarchical theory, but by a disclosive metaphor of empirical objectivity attentive to the human making of history. It was, if you will, a shift from the perspective of an Aristotelian theory disclosed by wisdom (*theoria, sophia*) to an Aristotelian notion of production or making disclosed by technique (*poiesis, techne*). Theory and praxis increasingly came under the aegis of empirical technique.[24]

Ever more refined methods of empirical research, contextual interpretation, and historical criticism immensely increased our knowledge of the historical background and composition of biblical narratives and church doctrines. But these methods tended to be techniques that studied such narratives or dogmas as *products*, as complexes of information, the origins and meanings of which could be disclosed irrespectively of any religious stance of the researcher, interpreter, or historian. The gap between empirical rationality and religious assent widened as a succession of psychological (Freud), sociological (Comte, Marx), and historical-critical (Baur, Harnack, Wrede) approaches dissected Scripture and church doctrines as merely human, culturally conditioned products, abstracted from any living relationship with converted religious conduct or transformative praxis. To be sure, there wasn't much of the latter visible in theological or hierarchical circles as spirituality continued its retreat into a private pietism. Secularism spread, and coupled with an industrial revolution that had subsumed empirical science into technology, challenged a whole series of religious traditions besides Christianity.[25]

A beleaguered Catholicism condemned all this as Modernism, even though its own trusted theologians were treating church doctrines as products (albeit divinely revealed products—*depositum fidei*), applying to them the logical techniques of formal and virtual predication, explicit or implicit deduction.[26] So-called orthodoxy developed its own brand of the reliance on technique characteristic of Liberalism or Modernism. As the first World War disclosed how a technically enlightened humankind could put the products of its new knowledge at the service of its old unconverted and unrepentant conduct (praxis), neo-orthodoxy responded with its call to *metanoia*. Soon a series of mediational theologies (Bultmann, Teilhard de Chardin, Rahner, Tillich) made use of various historical ontologies to disclose creative relationships between the advances of empirical sciences or scholarly techniques and traditional religious doctrines.[27]

3. *A contemporary praxis enlightenment* has its origins in some nineteenth-century attempts to elaborate methods for the human sciences distinct from those of the natural sciences. The value-free pretensions of the modern technical enlightenment are criticized. Merely

disclosive models of truth are incomplete, for what is disclosed may well be the alienating falsehood of biased theories, techniques and human conduct (praxis) sedimented in repressive social structures. If praxis as specifically conscious human conduct is capable of deformed action when controlled exclusively by theories or techniques, that praxis still has imperative orientations to freedom which can be disclosed only through transformative actions in accord with the imperatives. The ultimate arbiter amid conflicting theories and techniques can only be found in such transformative praxis. The search for truth, then, has an intrinsic orientation to freedom and responsibility as it struggles in the present to discern meaning and value.[28] Far from belittling the disclosive achievements of the classical enlightenment, or the empirical methods of the modern enlightenment, this praxis enlightenment attempts to ground those achievements and methods in related and recurrent operations of social, intellectual, moral, and religious performance. It seeks to disclose their positive and negative aspects by adverting to norms inherent in transformative praxis.[29]

Church doctrines or dogmas are not seen as only hierarchically revealed truths, nor simply as socio-psychological or cultural products, but as memories subversive of unfreedom (Metz), as boundaries of ongoing educational traditions (Segundo), as sets of meanings and values informing individual and collective Christian living (Lonergan).[30] Theology becomes a critical co-worker with other sciences, scholarly disciplines, pastoral and social ministries. Together they seek to disclose and transform the concrete personal, communal, social, political, and cultural life-forms within which Christians live out, or fail to live out, the transformative memories and values of their traditions. The objectivity of the truth of dogmas is conditioned by the transformative response of Christian praxis.[31]

Political theology, therefore, would see the criticisms of dogma by Berger, Tracy, Voegelin, and Welte as somewhat misplaced. The disclosive categories of a phenomenology, an ontology, or a sociology of knowledge tend to overlook the ortho-practical foundations of dogmas: the imperatives to change which they express. It is not sufficient to oppose doctrinal symbols to the experiential symbols of biblical narratives. For the latter, no less than the former, are in danger of congealing into static forms if their imperatives for transformation are not lived out in practice. Orthodoxy as 'speaking the truth' is grounded in, and oriented toward, orthopraxy as 'doing the truth.'

Attention to the transformative dimensions of dogma can be found in B. Lonergan's *The Way to Nicea: The Dialectical Development of Trinitarian Theology* and in his essay on 'The Origins of Christian Realism.'[32] There are also E. Peterson's studies on how the Trinitarian and Christological doctrines expressed and called for a spirituality at odds with the centralizing ambitions of Roman Imperial authority.[33] The relevance of these dogmas for our contemporary experience, the imperatives with which they challenge us, are expressed in the German Synod's *Confession of Faith in Hope* written by J. B. Metz: they are explored in J. Segundo's *Our Idea of God,* F. Fiorenza's essay on 'Critical Social Theory and Christology', and in other recent studies of the transformative dimensions of Christian living.[34] Much more work needs to be done. We have to know if, and how, church doctrines of the past brought Christian living critically to bear on the economic, social, and political conditions of their times. Unlike the historical analyses made under the aegis of modern enlightenment techniques, such studies, while using those techniques of historical scholarship, would not simply reduce doctrines to the plausibility structures of their historical context. Such reductionism would not do justice to the life-forms of those who lived the doctrines. Instead those studies would indicate if, and how, the dogmas expressed and promoted a praxis critical of the plausibility structures insofar as these hindered intellectual, moral, social, and/or religious development. To what extent are dogmas expressive of a knowledge born of transformative religious love—a 'love that is not to be just words or mere talk, but something real and active', a love 'only by which we can be certain that we belong to the realm of the truth' (1 Jn 3:18 f.)? Insofar as dogmas are such a knowledge and we fail to live by them, our experience will be anathema.

## Notes

1. P. Berger, 'Zur Soziologie kognitiver Minderheiten', in *Internationale Dialog Zeitschrift,* 2 (1969), pp. 127-32; id. *A Rumor of Angels* (New York, 1969); J. Metz, ed., 'Perspectives of a Political Ecclesiology', in *Concilium* 66 (1971), pp. 7-23, 35-49, 50-81. Berger's undifferentiated two-kingdom theology is evident in his 'Secular Theology and the Rejection of the Supernatural', in *Theol. Studies* 38 (19-77), pp. 39-56.

2. E. Voegelin, *The Ecumenic Age (Order and History* IV) (Baton Rouge, 1974), pp. 48, 259-71.

3. Ibid., p. 48.

4. Ibid., pp. 261-62.

5. B. Welte, 'Die Lehrformel von Nikaia und die abendländische Metaphysik', id. (ed.), *Zur Frühgeschichte der Christologie* (Freiburg in Br., 1970), pp. 100-107.

6. D. Tracy, *Blessed Rage for Order* (New York, 1975), pp. 64-87, 172-236.

7. Ibid., 242-26.

8. Cf. P. Berger, *The Sacred Canopy* (New York, 1967); id., *A Rumor of Angels,* pp. 76 ff.; Voegelin, op. cit., pp. 2-58; Welte, *Auf der Spur des Ewigen* (Freiburg, 1965), pp. 211-76, 380-426; Tracy, op. cit., pp. 111-71.

9. M. Lamb, 'The Theory-Praxis Relationship in Contemporary Christian Theologies', in *Catholic Theol. Society of America Proceedings* 31 (1976), pp. 149-78; id., *History, Method and Theology* (Missoula, 1977), pp. 2-114.

10. Ibid., pp. 19-52, 479-536.

11. B. Lonergan, *Method in Theology* (New York, 1972), pp. 125-45.

12. Berger, *Rumor*, pp. 52-75; Tracy, op. cit., pp. 92-4; Voegelin, op. cit., 6-11; Welte, *Im Spielfeld von Endlichkeit und Unendlichkeit* (Frankfurt, 1967).

13. Berger, *Rumor*, pp. 61-4; Tracy, op. cit., pp. 210-11, 237-40, 244; Voegelin, op. cit., pp. 2-6, 333-35; Welte, *Dialektik der Liebe* (Frankfurt, 1973), pp. 49-63.

14. Cf. Metz, 'Political Theology, in *Sacramentum Mundi* III (London, 1970), cols. 1232-40; id., *Theology of the World* (London, 1969) 89 ff., 99-116; Lamb, 'Les implications méthodologiques de la théologie politique, in M. Xhaufflaire (ed.), *La pratique de la théologie politique* (Tournai, 1974), pp. 51-70; J. Moltmann, *The Crucified God* (New York, 1974) (Der Gekreuzigte Gott Munich, 1973); Metz, 'Erlösung und Emanzipation', in L. Scheffczyk (ed.), *Erlösung und Emanzipation* (Freiburg, 1973), pp. 120-40; H. Peukert, *Wissenschaftstheorie—Handlungstheorie—Fundamentale Theologie* (Düsseldorf, 1976); J. Segundo, *The Liberation of Theology* (Maryknoll, 1976) (*Liberación de la teología*, Buenos Aires, 1975); Lonergan, op. cit., pp. 3-55; id. 'Theology and Praxis', in *Catholic Theol. Society of America Proceedings*, 32 (1977), pp. 1-20.

15. Cf. J. Ritter, *Metaphysik und Politik* (Frankfurt, 1969); R. Bernstein, *Praxis and Action* (Philadelphia, 1971), pp. 11-83; J. Habermas, *Theory and Praxis* (Boston, 1973) (*Theorie und Praxis*, Frankfurt, 1971); K.-O. Apel, *Transformation der Philosophie*, vol. II (Frankfurt, 1973), pp. 9-27, 9-154; Lamb, *History, Method and Theology*, pp. 56-114.

16. Cf. A. Wellmer, *Critical Theory of Society* (New York, 1971) (*Kritische Gesellschaftstheorie und Positivismus*, Frankfurt 1969); D. Böhler, *Metakritik der Marxschen Ideologiekritik* (Frankfurt, 1971); J. O'Neill (ed.), *On Critical Theory* (New York, 1976).

17. Cf. Lonergan, *Insight: A Study of Human Understanding* (New York, 1957), pp. 174-75, 286-87, 289-91, 713-18; G. Baum, *Man Becoming* (New York, 1971).

18. Cf. C. Lenhardt, 'The Wanderings of Enlightenment', in J. O'Neil (ed.), op. cit., pp. 34-57; Metz, Moltmann, Oemüller, *Religion and Political Society* (New York, 1974) (*Kirche in Prozess der Aufklärung*, Mainz 1970); Habermas, op. cit., pp. 253-305.

19. Cf. M.-D. Chenu, *La théologie comme science au XIIIe siècle* (Paris, 1943); L.-B. Geiger, *La participation dans la philosophie de S. Thomas d'Aquin* (Paris, 1953); H. Parkes, *The Divine Order* (New York, 1969); J. Wright, *The Order of the Universe in the Theology of St Thomas Aquinas* (Rome, 1957).

20. T. Aquinas, *Summa Theologiae*, II-II, 2, 6-8; this hierarchical ordering also affected Aquinas's understanding of prudence, ibid., II-II, 47, 12.

21. Cf. J. Hochstaffl, *Negative Theologie* (Darmstadt, 1976); B. Lonergan, *Verbum: Word and Idea in Aquinas* (Notre Dame, 1967); J. Metz, *Christliche Anthropozentrik* (Munich, 1962).

22. Cf. P. Gay, *The Enlightenment* (New York, 1966), pp. 242 ff.; F. Copleston, *Late Medieval and Renaissance Philosophy* (New York, 1963), vol. I, pp. 74-107, 132 f., 193-218; vol. II, 37-54; K. Michalski, *La philosophie au XIVe siècle*, ed., K. Flasch (Frankfurt, 1969).

23. Cf. T. Sanks, *Authority in the Church: A Study in Changing Paradigms* (Missoula, 1974); M. Seckler, 'Die Theologie als kirchliche Wissenschaft nach Pius XII. und Paul VI.', in *Tübinger Theol. Quartalschrift,* 149 (1969), pp. 209-34.

24. Cf. H. Barnes, *A History of Historical Writing* (New York, 1962), pp. 136-276; on Ranke's notion of power as disclosive of freedom, cf. H.-G. Gadamer, *Truth and Method* (New York, 1975) (*Wahrheit und Methode,* Tübingen, 1965), pp. 178-87; on the empiricist fallacy underlying the notion of 'making' history, cf. Lamb, *History, Method and Theology,* pp. 73-92, 120-36, 249-54, 341-56; on the pervasiveness of technique, cf. J. Ellul, *The Technological Society* (New York, 1964) (*La technique ou l'enjeu du siècle,* Paris, 1954).

25. Cf. Habermas, 'Dogmatism, Reason, and Decision: On Theory and Praxis in Our Scientific Civilization, in op. cit., pp. 253-82; Lamb, *History*, pp. 459-78; H. Frei, *The Eclipse of Biblical Narrative* (New Haven, 1974); J. Walgrave, *Unfolding Revelation* (Philadelphia, 1972), pp. 179-253.

26. Ibid., pp. 135-78; G. McCool, *Catholic Theology in the Nineteenth Century* (New York, 1977); W. Schulz, *Dogmenentwicklung als Problem der Geschichtlichkeit der Wahrheitserkenntnis* (Rome, 1969), pp. 71-124.

27. Cf. P. Barthel, *Interprétation du langage mythique et théologie biblique* (Leiden, 1963); W. Pannenberg, *Philosophy of Science and Theology* (Philadelphia, 1976) (*Wissenschaftstheorie und Theologie,* Frankfurt, 1973), pp. 29-224.

28. Cf. G. Picht, *Wahrheit, Vernunft, Verantwortung* (Stuttgart, 1969), pp. 108-40, 183-202, 281-407.

29. Cf. Lonergan, *Method,* pp. 235-93; Peukert, op. cit., pp. 250-323; E. Becker, *The Structure of Evil* (New York, 1968).

30. Cf. Metz, 'Erinnerung', *Handbuch phil. Grundbegriffe,* vol. 2 (Munich, 1973), pp. 386-98; id., 'The Future in the Memory of Suffering', *Concilium* 76 (1972), pp. 9-25; Segundo, op. cit., pp. 175-81; Lonergan, *Method,* pp. 311-20.

31. Cf. Lonergan, *Grace and Freedom* (New York, 1971), pp. 80-92, 103-9; id., *De Constitutione Christi Ontologica et Psychologica* (Rome, 1961), pp. 51-56.

32. Bernard Lonergan, *The Way to Nicea* (Philadelphia, 1976); id., 'The Origins of Christian Realism', in *A Second Collection* (Philadelphia, 1974), pp. 239-61. Both these writings attempt to show how the development of doctrine was not simply the result of the impact of Graeco-Roman conceptuality upon Christianity.

33. E. Peterson, 'Der Monotheismus als politisches Problem, and, Christus als Imperator', in *Theologische Traktate* (Munich, 1951), pp. 45-147, 150-64.

34. J. Segundo, *Our Idea of God* (Maryknoll, 1974) (*Nuestra idea de Dios,* Buenos Aires, 1970); F. Fiorenza, 'Critical Social Theory and Christology', *Catholic Theol. Society of America Proceedings* 30 (1975), pp. 63-110; J. Metz, *Followers of Christ* (London & New York, 1978); S. Moore, *The Crucified Jesus is No Stranger* (New York & London, 1977); J. Shea, *Stories about God* (Chicago, 1977).

# PART IV

*The Theology of Experience Related to Experience*

Carlo Molari

# The Hermeneutical Rôle of the Christian Community on the Basis of Judaeo-Christian Experience

THE CHURCH has to solve the problem of how to give a good account of her own history. It should be the story of the Church during all time and carry the meaning of her continual mission. This is much more difficult during times of rapid cultural change because of the call for readjustment and re-interpretation.

The real question here, among all the problems which arise in interpreting the traditions of religion and which remind us of the events of revelation, is where does the vital significance of the culture being handed on come from.

This part of the problem should not be identified with the official organ (the magisterium) or any of the specific institutions dedicated to interpretation (theological colleges and seminaries). Both work on the meaningfulness of a life of faith and take from that the right to cast themselves in a hermeneutical rôle, as interpreters of tradition; it is the community that welcomes it and lives it out in a variety of historical situations.

PRE-SUPPOSITIONS

Some preliminary data justify this assumption.

## The identity of the Church

The Christian Church comes into its own through tradition. It begins with the historical Jesus of Nazareth, at which time it was rooted in

Judaism, and it has developed by means of many other cultural contributions. It is not enough, nowadays, to define the community in terms of its beginnings and of the will of Christ. The Christian community today can only arrive at a sense of identity by learning about its history and traditions.

## Traditional means

A cultural tradition is a social structure, the result of a continuous series of interactions, and it becomes like that 'only when objectified into a system of symbols of some kind, and when the objectification can repeat the communal experience'.[1]

In the Judaeo-Christian tradition this came about in forms which had great influence on society. Language plays a primary rôle in the Christian tradition through dogmatic formulas, readings from the Bible, and the many rituals which use words. A second way in which the tradition has become part of society is figurative. Images fixed, preserved and transmitted the emotive objects and showed people how to behave. Other than in some other traditional religions, such as Islam or primitive Judaism or Buddhism, the figurative in Christianity has always played an important part in the establishing of the tradition. In certain periods of history, religious images have been the only examples for whole communities.

Ritual gestures constitute another way in which tradition is established. It is not just the events themselves, but their essential meaning, which one is also reminded of by watching the rites. The constant repetition of symbolic gestures is a means of indicating ways of behaviour which have matured over the centuries.

Modes of behaviour and the rules and regulations attached to them are the usual means whereby vital experience is transmitted to a social group or to a community.

By living in a certain pre-determined way people accept the ideals which fit in with them and then demonstrate their value.

## Revelatory events

Any cultural tradition reminds one of the events on which it is based. It refers, for instance, to episodes in history which are constant, in terms of experience, and which reveal their vital quality and constitute answers to the problems of living.

Even when a tradition formulates itself into formal doctrines, or tangible images, in commemorative rituals and moral precepts, it is still performing the function of remembering facts.

Tradition is steeped in historic experience even when it is not retelling history in so many words.

Judaeo-Christianity has preserved its characteristics by the formulation of an immediate and original faith. One has only to consider the Hebrew forms: 'A Syrian ready to perish was my father . . .' (Deut 26:5-10); or the language of Christianity in 'The God of our fathers raised up Jesus whom you slew and hanged on a tree . . . We are the witness of these things and so also is the Holy Spirit who God hath given to them that obey him' (Acts 5:30-1). These words transmit tradition because the forms of faith remind one of revelation, happenings which help us to understand more about human existence and which result in vitally significant ways of behaving.

## Differing areas of interpretation

In interpreting a religious tradition it is not enough simply to recount previous experience; we must also make sense of it. It is not enough to know what happened, we must also learn the vital meaning of the experience. It is not enough to ask how the strands in the tradition came into being or what the motives were behind the introduction of them, or how they were interpreted over the centuries: we must also ask what their usefulness is and how they answer real and present need and how they seem in the light of basic everyday problems. A religious tradition must aim first and foremost at making sense of life before contemplating the thoughts of the elders or the intentions of the narrators.

When it turns out that a cultural tradition is fixated in ritual, moral codes, in reported accounts and in formulas, interpretation of them cannot be limited to a socio-historical analysis. The great value of a tradition is that it should not only be discoverable in a version of history (although this can be very useful) but that it should also reveal 'symptoms of vitality'.

### DYNAMIC DEVELOPMENTS IN TRADITION

The need to pass on a tradition is linked to the very way in which that is done. It is done by means of symbolic outlines which cry out for an accompanying interpretation and imply the need for hermeneutical aid.

A cultural tradition is not handed on merely by using material that has already been gathered. It requires a continual process of justification and explanation.

The hermeneutical aspect of a cultural tradition is to be seen in the very acts and moments in time when they take place. Whether they come in verbal phrases or figures loaded with emotion, or are rituals or ways of behaving which are habitual, the handing-on process uses modules which are in continual need of explanation. It falls to the interpretative capacity of the subject to whom one wishes to transmit the cultural heritage.

Seen in this light, culture is 'a collection of working outlines, with interpretations, round which a group of human beings organizes its activity and which gives a "face" to its world and a sense of purpose to life'.[2]

Differing hermeneutical requirements are made by the announcements or figures or pieces of behaviour used. In some cases it is enough simply to understand what is in front of one and in others it is a question of adapting it, and in yet others it is a matter of putting new light on received formulas. In the scientific circles typical of our society the transmission of new ideas and principles is directed towards further discoveries and towards a wider and more universal application, with a view to stimulating new theories. Their tradition leads them to being characterized as 'inventive'; it asks for a new hermeneutical attitude which penetrates the more static elements in the tradition.

These dynamic approaches look into all aspects of the symbolic structure in question.

*Semiotics*

The need for interpretative processes in the handing down of a tradition arises, above all, from the collective meaning of the standard.

Standards wear out in time, they lose their meaning; they get used up and have to be renewed. To keep their meaning, a cultural community has to invent new ways of handing on the whole content of its tradition.

This process, however, is not achieved by a series of crises. Both psychological and social factors play a part in this very complex process. Serious and constructive criticism must analyze the meaning of every symbol rigorously. All the twists and turns in the production of symbols must be examined so as to reveal every last hidden aspect of them. In other words, it is necessary to 'go back along the way in which the symbol was produced', 'to disentangle certain meaningful procedures from their specific place and historical source', and to 'find out more about their 'topicality'. Everything should be dealt with in this way: 'pronouncements, the organization, grammar and knowledge, so as to reach the area in which the seeds lie that have a meaningful presence in the language'.[3] In that way it should be possible to find out the reasons why a word, or a figure, or a gesture take on, or lose, value, and the way in which they change or keep their meaning.

If this were done, it would be possible to set a value on all attempts to single out the formative aspects of symbols at an unconscious and a conscious level. They must be archetypal (to use Jung's terminology), in which case the language has condensed mankind's experience in the past and translated it into a symbol. A study of their provenance may throw a field of analysis open to theology and this could amount to relevant conclusions in the matter of doctrine. It would mean a radical hermeneutic role which has its roots in anthropology and which would have the whole community as carrier and vital interpreter of its values in the formation of symbols.

So it is with the introduction of new symbols: in linguistics, picture-making and gestures they are in themselves hermeneutical acts. It implies a process of interpretation of the vital contents which they are interested in preserving and carrying on. What is needed is confirmation of the efficacy of the symbol in the living situation.

The Christian tradition can furnish many examples of crises of meaningful structure which have resulted in the need to look for effective new symbols. These crises often come at the same time as a recognition of the uselessness of the signs, and that gives rise to new expressive forms which complete them and substitute words for them in common use without negating what has gone before. The various 'symbols' of faith came into being through just such a situation.

This happens not only in language but to other symbolic forms which undergo this process.

The West has not given such canonical importance to pictorial symbols as has been the case in eastern communities. Perhaps that is exactly the reason why western images of faith have developed with a greater degree of variety and richness. In the East the shaping of the figures is subject to very rigorous rules and regulations, and their interpretation follows rules which are extremely detailed and fixed.[4]

The liturgical revival has gone forward in a different rhythm in the two halves of the world. The fundamental reason for the changes came about for the same cause, however; the symbols were worn out and were no longer able to pass on the meaning of what happened in history with any immediacy or in a simple way.

## Semantics

Not only meanings can wear out but what is actually said: that is, the cultural content of what is handed on goes through a process of deterioration and is under continual pressure. One might even say that the life of the meanings is in itself much more vulnerable than the systems and rules for the expression of them. The value set on, and the place found for, a cultural element and given a verbal 'meaning', or an image or a mode of behaviour, is determined not only by the symbol used but by the position they occupy in the whole cultural system.

Thus the introduction of new cultural elements (a scientific discovery, for example, or a new historical happening, and so on) might change all the meanings in a particular system, even without bringing in a specific new symbol.

That is why sociologists have observed that, today more than ever, changes in the cultural system have speeded up; 'the life of a study of meanings seems to last no longer than that of pronunciation, the organization of which remained unchanged for centuries in the history of the language'.[5]

Within the Christian tradition these facts are particularly observable and call for constant re-interpretation.[6] Because of this, the declaration *Mysterium ecclesiae* (24 June 1973) asserted the validity and significance of the forms of the dogma from earlier times, reminded one of their network of 'interpretation' and 'comprehension', and admitted that 'so as to stay alive and fruitful in habitual usage of the Church', it must look for 'timely expository and explicatory additions, which maintain and clarify its inner meaning'.[7] To explain that need, the document itself outlines the difficulty encountered in talking about revelation, a difficulty that exists quite apart from the inherent mystery in the subject, and which comes from 'the historical conditioning which results in the ways of expressing revelation' because of which 'the sense of the pronouncements *depends, to some extent, on the peculiar expressiveness of a language in use at a certain time and in a given set of circumstances.*[8]

These features are linked to incessant changes in contemporary culture of the forms (analogous to the figures, rites and ways of behaving), and put pressure on a cultural community to interpret their tradition continuously so as to hand it on with a certain degree of coherence.

## The hermeneutical element

The same conclusion can be arrived at by analyzing what is done to hand on a cultural tradition in different places, and the interpretative modes they use.

*Translation.* The history of a cultural tradition is one of continual translation. As its cultural horizons change, in terms of history and geography, a social group finds itself obliged to translate its own culture so as to pass it on. These days a translation does not come through a verbal transliteration. By using a language, indeed, one is already in the business of using a preconceived view of the world, albeit reduced to verbal schemes along with a syntax and a vocabulary. To go from one language to another requires a delicate transfusion from one semantic system to another. A semantic system is 'a way of giving shape to the world. And as such it is a partial interpretation of the world itself and can always be restructured when new facts arise and bring about a crisis'.[9]

If there were a universal semantic system, there would be no need for translations. If there were a permanent semantic system such changes would not have to be gone through, thus upsetting whole sectors of a culture. The content would be communicated without having to go to the length of a translation. Any translation presupposes a reference to reality as interpreted according to the particular code in use.

When it comes to Christian faith it is not possible to think in terms of a translation without referring to the basic facts of revelation. They constitute the ultimate 'reference' for every formula of faith. It is not what is said (meaning), but what is spoken about in several different ways (salvation) which is the reality the community refers to when it wants to translate its faith. Formulas of Christian faith have come from Aramaic to Greek to Latin, and from them to modern languages. But the Christian faith has not yet been translated properly into African or Indian or reached the Far East from the western languages. That is the task before our generation. We have the opportunity to put a new interpretation on salvation in the semantic modes of those cultures.

*Means of interpretation.* Within our own culture over the years one can find many different ways of interpreting the salvation. A significant way has been to imitate an exegesis of Scripture. Now that the day of the exegesis in historico-critical terms in religious development is over, attempts are being made to use psycho-sociological methods. Bible stories told in a primitive symbolic language are a rich mine for psychological analysis. Other stories can be seen in a sociological light. This method is applied to the history of dogma, and may result in more opportunities for recourse to hermeneutics, which is not yet as solidly established as the historical methods were a century ago.

## HERMENEUTICAL METHODS

In order to communicate a tradition it must necessarily be adapted to real life and so translated and interpreted. A community which has a culture looks for hermeneutical means.

## Socialization

The handing on of a tradition involves various people in a profound and vital relationship which is the process of socialization. This can be seen happening very well in primary socialization. This comes about through the very people who give life in the first phase of human existence, and is made actual in circumstances loaded with strong emotions. 'There is a good deal of reason to believe that without the emotional attachment to people that influences children, the process of learning would be very difficult, if not impossible'.[10] During this time language is learned and used. It is also a means of socialization. Language is the means of interpretation and communication. It interprets and communicates a sense of the values interwoven in the traditional culture.[11]

Albeit in a different form, these mechanisms work towards the development of relationships which result in mature socializations: thus a community enables its members to grow up, and passes on values, rules, attitudes and ways of behaving.

This results in the adoption of new habits and of specific vocabularies, and of universally accepted and understood semantics. 'The second level of socialization requires the learning of a vocabulary connected to rôles, which means, at first at any rate, the interiorization of semantics which structure the *interpretation* and the conduct of *routines* within an institution. At this time the "silent meanings" are also learnt, along with the values and the effective "colouring" of these areas of semantics . . . In order to establish and preserve coherence, the second phase of socialization presupposes conceptual procedures which incorporate different bodies of knowledge'. [12]

## Socialization within the faith

The processes of socialization within the faith follow the laws outlined by the sociology of consciousness, but concentrates principally on the function of the social group.

*Witness.* Witness is an essential feature of the faith. It makes ideals which are otherwise unacceptable, acceptable. The community provides a structure of certainty. Through it, one can establish the validity of a selected group of historical stories, the saving aim of attitudes, rules and values which are put forward as absolute.

In choices made in life it is not possible to validate ideals before having lived them. At the moment of choice we have the witness of others to demonstrate them to us. Witness ought not to be reduced to mere verbal testimony, nor to simple moral impositions. It should consist of an inducement to good behaviour and to learning of values through propinquity. By living out an ideal and showing it in our lives in a positive way we are able to communicate it to others.

The community in all its various authentic ways bears witness to the faith. Each one of us, in his way, bears witness and that unites all those all over the world who believe in chosing the fundamental, meaningful values in life. To bear witness without taking in all aspects of human life, to limit oneself to certain aspects, cannot be considered as truly bearing witness. It must incorporate all aspects of life.

That is why bearing witness to religious faith is necessarily a community activity. The meaning of salvation can only be seen through a multiplicity of living situations.

*The Sacraments.* The liturgy is another important way in which we hand down the traditions of the faith. By means of various symbols it reminds us of the ideals we have chosen and renews our adherence to them in a gesture of participation. The sacraments call for symbolic gestures through which the ecclesiastical community acknowledges and expresses the existence of the means of salvation offered by God through Christ, and accepts the duty of testifying to it.

It is for this reason that the sacraments accompany the various stages of socialization within the faith from first communion to the last rites. The gift of life is comforting and one is handing it on to another in a continual exchange. Life presupposes and builds a sense of unity.

The ecclesiastical community defines 'The universal sacrament of salvation' (LG 48) as 'the symbol and the instrument of intimate union with God and unity with the whole human race.' (LG I).

## The ecclesiastical community as hermeneutic

All the aspects that we have analyzed show that in fact the ecclesiastical community is the active element in socialization within the faith. It carries the burden of interpreting tradition. The whole community hands down the tradition, witnesses to the faith, and interprets both for the coming generation.

It cannot be otherwise; no tradition of faith could be carried down the centuries without an alert people.

The validity of choice cannot be verified unless a community expresses itself in a variety of ways and lives in various cultural situations.

A savific tradition, such as Judaeo-Christianity is, is not accidental but is an intrinsic part of the community. It cannot be handed down or interpreted unless in harmony and progressively throughout its history.

This is quite clear even when we consider the founding of Judaeo-Christian revelation. The documents which have been handed down to us are the outcome of a continuous re-reading of the original events. There is not one important event in the Jewish story nor any pronouncement made by a prophet which has not been re-read, albeit in varying conditions, and interpreted again with the deepest possible meaning.

The New Testament itself consists of an adaptation of the interpretation of the message of life and of the person of Jesus taken from the Acts of the Apostles and the early Christian community. The living faith means going over and re-interpreting the story of salvation, which concerns all the people of God.

## VARIOUS HERMENEUTICAL FUNCTIONS

There have to be various rôles within the community of the faithful. And each of them carries a hermeneutical responsibility. There are scholars and linguists and historians, like the scribes, Pharisees and theologians. There is the service of the magisterium which authenticates the interpretations made in the living community. There is the service given by unofficial people who are particularly suited to interpretations through art or doctrine, or, most important of all, questions of daily living. Prophets used to have, and in some ways still do have, great importance in the Judaeo-Christian tradition.

### The prophets

They are often the best interpreters of salvation. They stir people out of their laziness; they rebuke the rich for their selfishness, and condemn the injustice of the powerful. But they too can only be understood in terms of an experience for the whole community. They express a tradition (even when they are not part of a school) and they are the bearers of wisdom from which the history of the whole people is originated. They give a voice to those who have none, those who are despised, weak and the dispossessed. They take up the forgotten words of the old prophets and the promises of the fathers which have not been kept; the gifts given, but neglected. They identify the meaning of what the community has experienced and at the same time they put on record the mature beliefs that have grown up during the long history of their people. Thus they speak in the name of God in that they live out their work by telling the story of salvation. Neither Judaism nor Christianity has placed much stress officially on the extempory and individual pronouncements made by the prophets. On the contrary, those who spoke according to their own instinct and from their own spirit became known as false prophets (cf. Jer 23:9; Ezek 13: 1-23). Jesus, too, was thought of as a prophet by his contemporaries (Mt 21:10; Mk 6:15; Lk 7:16; 9.8; Jn 9:17). The name, however, is one of the most characteristic features of Judaeo-Christianity. Jesus was willing to recognize his own rôle as a prophet (cf. Mt 13:57; Lk 13:33) and looked forward to a fate like those of the prophets (cf., Mt 23:37-8). The prophets played an important part in early Christian communities; they declared the will of God as it was in various situations, exhorted and comforted, stimulated and rebuked. Paul compares a prophet to one who speaks in an unknown language; while he is indeed not understood, his message is understood even by those who are not among the faithful (I Cor 14:3, 24). Each generation of Christians has had its prophets; they were those who extracted the true moments from historical events and gave them an interpretation. They were not always listened to, and sometimes not even believed in, but history has justified them. They were not always perfect men but wisdom flowed from their words for the whole community, and they were the fruits of holiness. Each one of the faithful has differing degrees of charisma, yet the community as a whole favours the emergence of the prophets and their activities so that the living meaning of experience shall not be lost to the Church. The prophets did not make it their business to 'create' interpretations of history; they simply had the sensitivity which enabled them to collect whatever had been lived through in history. Their intuitions proved rich and faithful, and their upsetting words proved to have a profound significance. Otherwise they passed unnoticed.

## The guarantee of hermeneutical authenticity—sanctity

Prophets need to have their pronouncements confirmed. It is sanctity alone which affords an intrinsic and authentic interpretation. The salvific tradition is faithfully received when it flourishes in the shape of a saintly life. The interpretation that can be seen in a saintly life has no further need of confirmation. First and last, a saint makes his actions bear out his ideals in life. 'Men do not make mistakes over sanctity. They recognize it at first sight by instinct as though they were attracted to it right away. It is proof unto itself without any need for critical support. It is the truth of the Gospel which has sustained and nourished it and the spirit of it can be recognized directly and spontaneously. It comes about because sanctity, the Gospel and God are one and the same thing'.[13] For this reason the criterion by which false prophets are judged is not in terms of a profession of faith in Christ (because they have often testified in his name (see Mt 7:22), nor can it be done by miracles (cf. Mk 13:22; Acts 13:13, etc.), but it can only be seen in all their behaviour and the fruits of the spirit of sanctity which grow in their vicinity (see Mt 7:16); their words destroy, whereas the true prophet builds. Prophetic pronouncements must be justified by sanctity. Only those who, even if they are not blessed with the charisma of a prophet, are sanctified within the ecclesiastical community and become the immediate criterion whereby a true interpretation of the word of God may be judged. They are those who are charged with being effectively hermeneutical in the Judaeo-Christian tradition descended from the salvation concentrated in the cumulative revelations made by Jesus Christ.

*Translated by A. Weir*


## Notes

1. P. L. Berger & T. Luckmann, *The Social Construction of Reality* (New York, 1966).

2. E. Riverso, *Individuo, societa, e cultura* (Rome, 1971), p. 13.

3. See O. Ducrot & T. Todorov, *Dictionaire encyclopédique des sciences du language* (Paris, 1972). See especially the pages on 'semanalysis' by J. Kristeva.

4. The manuals for composing figures were always seen as 'hermeneutical'; that is, interpretative. The most famous is the *Guida alla pittura de Monte Athos* written by Dionigi di Furna (1745), edited by A. N. Didron in 1845. The title is *Ermeneia tes zographikes teknes*. The classic view of iconography was that it was not made by the imagination but that it was a process of revelation; the artist was bringing to light in the wood an eternal image made by God. Because of this, there is a common expression in Russian 'raskyvat obraz', to *discover* a painting is the same as saying 'create or compose' a painting. Cf. *Prolegomeni al tema della Semiotica dell'icona*. An interview with Boris Uspenski of Zbigniew Podgorzec in *Znak* no. 12 (1976). See also M. Alpatove, *Le iconi russe*. Problems in the history of artistic interpretation (Turin, 1976), trans. from the Russian.

5. U. Eco *Trattato di semiotica generale* (Milan, 1975), pp. 359-60.

6. A simple example in theology is provided by the sudden change in the word 'persona'. Nowadays its use in connection with the Trinity has become almost trite, while Christology tends to make it monotheistic. Long explanatory notes are needed to avoid these errors. Cf. observations by K. Rahner in *Mysterium salutis* (Einsiedeln, 1967), on the Trinity and *persona*. On Christology see K. Rahner, *Grundkurs des Glaubens* (Freiburg, 1976).

7. 'His consideratis, dicendum est formulas dogmaticas Magisterii Ecclesiae veritatem revelatam ab initio apte comunis asse et, manentes easdem, eam in

perpetuum comunicatures esse recte *interpretantibus* ipsas' AAS 65 (1973), 403; (the whole document occupies pp. 396-408).

8. Ibid., p. 407.

9. U. Eco, op. cit., pp. 359-60.

10. P. L. Berger & T. Luckmann, op. cit., p. 102. He adds in the notes, 'It was the advances made by Freudians in infant psychology that revealed this capacity to learn and certain theories of behaviour have confirmed them. What I am saying is not intended to be taken as acceptance of any of the theories held by any schools of psychology' (ibid., n. 5).

11. See E. Wulff on the nature of Vietnamese culture as seen in language in *Psychiatrie und Klassengesellschaft* (Frankfurt, 1972). He deals in particular with the collective ideal shown by the Vietnamese language in that 'it renounces personal and possessive pronouns and uses verbs in the infinitive only. There are no tenses, conjugations and no distinction between active and passive moods'.

12. P. L. Berger & T. Luckmann, op. cit., pp. 191, 193.

13. Y. Congar, in *Mysterium salutis,* IV/I (Einsiedeln, 1972).

David Tracy

# The Particularity and Universality of Christian Revelation

## REVELATION AND EXPERIENCE: THE NEW RESOURCES OF REVISED THEORIES OF HERMENEUTICS AND EXPERIENCE

IN THE recent past of liberal and neo-orthodox Christian theologies, the doctrine of revelation assumed a primary rôle, for reasons largely posed by the related problematics of epistemology and historical consciousness. From Troeltsch through Bultmann, Barth, and H. Richard Niebuhr among Protestant theologians, from the neo-scholastics through the earlier work of the phenomenological and/or transcendental Thomists, the doctrine of revelation was reformulated in distinct but related theologies of revelation. In retrospect, however—and with no disparagement of the permanent achievements of that extraordinary period in Christian theology—the concept of revelation in these theologies seems now too determined by legitimate but confining considerations for conceptual knowledge. The relationship of revelation to experience was present both implicitly and explicitly in these theologies. However, experience functioned in a secondary rôle in comparison to the problem of the need for universal concepts for a radically historical revelation.

The need for second-order, conceptual discourse for a doctrine of revelation was studied with care and precision. The contours of the actual first-order religious discourse of the Scriptures (prophetic, narrative, poetic, wisdom, proverbial, parabolic, letters, hymnic) were, with a few notable exceptions, left largely unthematized until the last fifteen years. The legitimate theological difficulties posed since Kant and Hegel on the exact relationships of *Vorstellung* and *Begriff* were decided largely in favour of a *Begrifflichkeit* now shorn of its Hegelian claims and related to different concepts of radical historicity. The concept of 'experience' itself, once so central to the doctrines of revelation of the earlier Catholic Modernists and Liberal Protestants, went relatively unexplored for these different theologies of revelation. To be sure, most Christian theologians abandoned the earlier and narrower approach to revelation focussing upon propositional truths in favour of a more dynamic, more personalist, more biblical, and, above all, more historically conscious approach to revelation as event. Still, the complex relationships between the first-order discourse of the Scriptures and the actual originating experience of revelation was noted but seldom thematized. The search for first-order discourse for new contemporary experiences of continuing revelation in our continuing history went similarly unthematized. Most attention was devoted to the second-order search for conceptualities more appropriate to the problematics of how to define the definitiveness of the originating revelation events in the context of a continuing history.

The concerns of historical consciousness—as epitomized in Ernst Troeltsch's classical formulation of the problematic of the 'absoluteness' of Christianity—united with the earlier epistemological and conceptual concerns to demand central attention from theologians. The theory of tradition as *traditio* expressed among Catholic theologians influenced by Blondel and Newman, and reformulated, more recently, by those hermeneutical theologians inspired by the philosopher Hans-Georg Gadamer served to challenge the two narrow confines of Enlightenment models of modernity, concept, symbol, and experience. Yet even this rich resource of *traditio* sometimes narrowed the discussion of revelation by assuming a merely negative stance against the Enlightenment. Nor did several of the theologies of revelation as tradition explicate the relationships between different order of language and experience in the continuing tradition.

The newer hermeneutical and socio-critical analyses of the last ten years, however, have provided fresh resources for understanding the relationships between revelation (whether originating or continuing) and experience. This newer hermeneutic has focussed its major attention upon first-order discourse, thereby allowing a theological retrieval of the originating religious discourse of the Scriptures. As witnessed, for example, in the work of Paul Ricoeur, this analysis has allowed the *referent* of this first-order discourse (that is, as referring to a possible-mode-of-being-in-the-world not 'behind' but 'in front of' the text) to emerge only after a careful hermeneutical analysis (including the use of literary-critical and structuralist methods) of the *sense* of different

genres. The analyses of the parables as both metaphor and narrative
are merely the best-known examples of these new hermeneutical en-
terprises. This same hermeneutics has allowed an understanding of the
complex relationships among such Old Testament first-order languages
for revelation as prophecy, narrative, *torah*, wisdom and hymnic discourse.

In sum, this hermeneutics has advanced the rethinking of the relationships between revelation and experience in three principal ways.
First, the analyses of the sense and referent of first-order discourse has
freed theologians to analyze the originating religious scriptural
language—the language closest to the original experience of
revelation—*before* proceeding to an analysis of second-order conceptual theological discourse (theologies *of* revelation). Second, the emphasis in hermeneutics upon the logicity of meaning in both sense and
referent as hermeneutically prior to the meaning of the author, the
context, or the original audience has been sound. In fact, this form of
hermeneutics has displaced any remaining romantic theories of interpretation from their once dominant position without sacrificing the
imperative demands of historicity. To try to employ some mysterious
form of 'empathy' to re-experience the author's experience or the original addressee's experience now seems a fruitless task for the actual
interpretation of the experiential meaning of the text. To interpret the
experiential referent of that text in direct relationship to the sense of
the text now seems the proper route for analyzing the actual revelatory
experiences disclosed by the first-order revelation-languages in the
Scriptures. Third, the emphasis upon the referent as a possible-mode-
of-being-in-the-world has focussed new attention upon the rôle of the
productive imagination in religious discourse and experience. In fact,
one may state that the concern with imagination of Kant's Third
Critique is now viewed as central for understanding revelation and
experience. This remains noticeably different from the dominant epistemological and ethical concerns of the first two critiques pervasively
present for earlier theologies of revelation. In sum, the recent forms of
hermeneutics inspired by Gadamer and Ricoeur have focussed on that
originating first-order religious discourse of the Scriptures in such a
manner that the originating religious experience *referred to* by the text
can be explicated without naive and romantic appeals to the interpreter's 'empathy' for the experience of the original author or for the
experience of the original addressee of the text.

Moreover, as the recent work of J. B. Metz and E. Schillebeeckx
among others have shown, one need not fear that this hermeneutical
emphasis upon the narrative core of Christian religious discourse over
later conceptualities will remove the socio-critical power of that first-

order discourse itself. The *memoria* of the suffering of the oppressed encapsulated in scriptural narratives, for example, assures that the memory of the *traditio* need never become merely conservative in the manner of some earlier theologies of revelation as tradition. For precisely that narrative core captures—as conceptual discourse alone cannot—the actual tensions of the disclosive and transformative power of the authentically Christian experience of God's revelation in the event of Jesus Christ as Lord.

These familiar, fruitful, largely European developments of hermeneutical and socio-critical analyses of the first-order scriptural discourse for the experience of revelation can be united, I believe, with the Anglo-American reformed notion of experience itself to provide new resources for the present question of revelation and experience.

European commentators sometimes assume that the Anglo-American emphasis upon experience in theology is at best merely common-sensical, at worst empiricist. The 'verification' and 'falsification' contributions of A. J. Ayer and Antony Flew may indeed lead one to this conclusion, as may some of the hermeneutically unsophisticated uses of story, symbol, and experience in some recent North American theologies. Still, the fact remains that a major Anglo-American tradition in philosophy and theology from Jonathan Edwards through William James, Charles Hartshorne, Alfred North Whitehead, the process theologies, and the various forms of Catholic and Protestant 'empirical theologies' have consistently argued against both conceptualism *and* empiricism in favour of a wider and deeper notion of experience itself. In one of his now classical formulations, Whitehead insisted upon the need for a reformed subjectivist principle. His insistence was not exhausted by the more widespread negative move against a Cartesian substance-subject in favor of a dynamic social subject-in-process. Rather, Whitehead also insisted (and here he was and is joined by all other philosophers and theologians in this empirical tradition) that the notion of experience employed in philosophy and theology was badly in need of revision beyond its conceptualist and empiricist confines. Our experience is not, in fact, confined to the reports of our five senses, much less to experimental verification (that is, to empiricism). Prior to all sense-experience is the primordial, pervasive experience of the self as a self: active, in process, feeling, embodied, intrinsically social, radically related to all reality. This primordial experience (technically, the feeling of non-sensuous perception) is always present to the self—a presence rendered consciously available through both elementary and sophisticated (for example, Lilly experiments) methods of consciousness-raising.

That same revised notion of experience both expands the candidates for experience beyond empiricist confines to feeling, mood, body awareness, time-space awareness, relations as experienced, and so on, and radicalizes the experience of the self as a self beyond both empiricist and conceptualist limitations. Indeed, as several theologians have attempted to show, the revised notion of experience also encourages a heightened awareness-experience of the whole as now frightening, now trustworthy, now fascinating, now terrifying. These latter experiences may be named limit-experiences. Certain of these limit-experiences (including not only the more familiar Jasperian negative limit-situations of anxiety, guilt, death, but the more positive limit-experiences of fundamental trust in a meaning and order to the whole) disclose a religious-as-limit dimension to our everyday experience distinct from and grounding to our cultural, scientific, ethical, and aesthetic experience.

In more secularized human beings, this limit-experience of a religious dimension to one's everyday existence sometimes serves as the sole clue to the character of religious experience and thereby to all personal appropriation of the languages of revelation (Whitehead's own urbane and secular spirit was probably of this cast). For others, more exactly for those who possess any genuine lived-experience of an authentically living religious *traditio* grounded in a revelation, the possibilities for experiential religion are wider, deeper, and far more intense than the earlier shared experience of a religious-as-limit dimension to the everyday. Christian revelation can be experienced by Christians living in a real religious community and an authentically revelatory tradition first in the form of what Mircea Eliade has analyzed as 'manifestations' (as in a vibrant sacramental life or in some of the new 'charismatic' experiences). That same intense experience of Christian revelation can also be found in what the kerygmatic theologians have analyzed as the faith experience of authentic proclamation. For Christians revelatory limit-experiences of both manifestation and proclamation are available in the authentic lived-experience of Church.

The same experience may be present, now in a reflectively mediated fashion, in the theological visions of the whole disclosed by the second-order languages of negative dialectics or of analogy (or, preferably both). In any case, the intensity of the Christian revelation-experience is disclosive not only of a religious dimension to one's existence but of intense religious experiences disclosed, nourished, and transformed by the originating revelatory experience of Jesus Christ. That originating experience is present more immediately through the proclamation and the manifestations of an authentic sacramental, ecclesial, life, including the struggle for justice in Church and world. That same experience is present in more mediated forms through the critical reflection present in the second-order discourse of theologians. It is further intensified by the continuing presence of authentic witnesses to the reality of revelation in the community (Mother Teresa, Dorothy Day, Dom Helder Camara). Yet these experiential resources for rethinking the doctrine of revelation are best rendered *theologically* (as distinct from religiously) available, once a theory of the hermeneutics of first-order discourse has been united with a theory of tradition which includes a socio-critical dimension. Both resources are further strengthened when united to a revised theory of experience which takes one beyond the confines of both conceptualism and empiricism. Still, these new resources may reformulate but do not resolve the full problematic of revelation and experience. For that, one must see what possible light they may bring to bear upon the still pressing questions of the character of explicitly Christian revelation.

## PARTICULARITY AND UNIVERSALITY IN CHRISTIAN REVELATION: CLASSIC TEXTS AND EVENTS

To employ these hermeneutical and experiential resources fruitfully for explicitly Christian revelation, the theologian must also find an explicit category with which to analyze the claims of distinct religious texts. First, however, a negative comment: the problem of Christian particularity in revelation should not be confused with claims to exclusivity. In fact, the mainline Catholic tradition in theology, with its frequent appeals to the universal salvific will of God, has been relatively unplagued in recent years by claims to exclusivity for Christian revelation. Still the need to understand when and how Christian particularity is neither particularism nor exclusivity but can be universal, decisive, and inclusivist needs further exploration with the new resources outlined in Part I.

In harmony with the notion of hermeneutics advanced above, a category worth exploring is the notion of the classic text. In approaching cultural texts, all civilized persons make certain assumptions. Chief among those assumptions are the following: first, there exists a qualitative difference between a classic and a period piece; second, there exists an assumption that a classic, by definition, will always be in need of further interpretation in view of its need for renewed application to a particular situation: third, a classic, again by definition, is assumed to be any text which always has the power to transform the horizon of the interpreter and thereby disclose new meaning and experiential possibilities.

Although these assumptions possess a firm empirical basis in any culture, there remains the theoretical difficulty of explicating criteria to distinguish between particularity and particularism, between universality and a mere universalism. One may reject romantic notions of the classic with their somewhat desperate appeals to 'genius' and individual taste while still insisting that the origins and genre of the genuine classic are always particular. For example, what could be more particular in origin and expression than James Joyce's *Ulysses,* a work expressing one day in the lives of three persons in Dublin (Bloomsday— June 16, 1904)? And yet that very particularity unites with a proper genre to disclose the universal relevance of this modern classic. The notion of a purely universalist literary classic is a notion best consigned to Enlightenment hopes become Enlightenment illusion. For the fact remains that all the great classics of our culture achieve their universality precisely through their particularity.

In the genuine classic, an unusual, even paradoxical tension of particularity and universality happens. First, there seems to occur an intensification-process in one's own experience. An individual explores the meaning of his/her own experience, own community, own tradition to that point of intensification wherein the desire for expression of the experience becomes necessity. At that point, a proper genre (poetry, narrative, autobiography, and so on) is discovered or invented to re-express (or imitate in its true sense of *mimesis* as imaginative re-description) that experience with force. Then all persons can imaginatively experience the feeling-tones, the meaning, the disclosure of this new possible mode-of-being-in-the-world. The traditional need for the presence-in-tension of both energy and form, both passion and *logos* becomes, in the analogous paradox of the classic, the presence-in-tension of particularity and universality. Indeed the universality of the classic text occurs only when a sufficiently passionate, intense particular experience is driven to find its form, its logos, its genre and its universality.

The religious classical text takes that same intensification process, that same alliance of *logos* with the risk of personal passion, a step further along the same intensification route. For then there occur those limit-experiences proper to religion and disclosive of, first, a religious dimension to our lives and then, yet more intensely, of the explicit religious experiences of a particular revelation tradition. The classical Hebrew and Christian religious texts find the proper expression of their religious experience in that first-order discourse expressed in the genres of narrative, prophecy, wisdom, hymn, parable and letter of the scriptures. Those genres do disclose, without loss of the full complexities and tensions of a religious passion united to *logos,* a genre-controlled referent. That referent remains a transformative revelatory experience expressive of the experiential contours, the paradoxical, challenging, even 'scandalous' and 'foolish' meanings of the Christian religious experience. These meanings are experienced as the now confronting, now appealing, always transformative Christian mode-of-being-in-the-world, radical faith, hope and agapic love.

Theological classical texts have the more difficult task of allowing a second-order, reflective discourse to enter more explicitly into both the process and the genre, and thereby the experience. When the theologian's more conceptual language maintains a fidelity to both the originating religious language and the equally passionate demands of the authentic interests of critical reason, the same process of intensification of personal particularity become disclosure of universality happens: For then, a new second-order discourse emerges to disclose through the mediation of reflection the same, now continuous and appealing, not discontinuous and confrontational Christian possibility for life.

As that master of suspicion upon all theological language, Søren Kierkegaard, insisted, the question of a proper genre for expressing authentic religious experience (for him indirect discourse through different genres and pseudonyms) is one too often overlooked by the 'theologians'. As Kierkegaard's own work also witnesses, the genre of passionate critical reflection is indispensable for the modern religious intellectual whose religious experience is more likely to be one of mediated second naïveté than one of immediate first naïveté.

Since even their most negative critics admit that the Old Testament and the New Testament contain classical religious texts, it seems fruitful to reformulate the problem of Christian particularity in the hermeneutical terms suggested above. For then we can witness how the Christian classics, like every classic, are indeed particular without being particularist, are in fact universal without being merely 'lowest common denominator' universalist. Indeed, the Scriptures serve for the Christian as the classic judging and transforming all other classics—the *norma normans non normata* of all Christian religious and theological language. Is this really so puzzling unless one is enamoured of a strange search for a universalism untouched by particularity? Indeed, to reject the highly particular experiences of passionate intensity which are the very life-blood of our lives because they are somehow assumed to be merely 'private' seems, at best, counterintuitive. Is one really to deny the deepest experiences of one's life—the experience of love for a particular person, the experience of religious nourishment in a particular community and tradition—because the experience seems somehow too particularist? Classical logos comes in and through passion; true form through energy; the right genre through the demands of intense personal, communal or traditional experience; the Apollinian experience of tragedy in and through the Dionysian; the universal in and through the particular. To remove that particularity is to remove the very possibility for a personal experience of religious intensification whereby the universal meaning of the experience may be disclosed.

The same kind of analysis holds when one shifts one's attention from the text to the person referred to by the text—as when one moves from the parables of Jesus to the Jesus referred to by the parables or by all the later texts of the New Testament confessing Jesus Christ as Lord. For the originating Christian religious texts consistently refer throughout their myriad of genres and formulations not only to the religious experience of the Christian (radical faith, hope and *agapic* love) but to this Jesus of Nazareth as the Christ, to this Christ as Lord, as disclosive, as revelatory, of the one true God who may now be recognized with all the force of a decisive revelation as Love. That event of God's revelation in Christ Jesus is the transformative event of a person in and through whose message, life, death, and resurrection the definitive revelation of both who we are and who God is decisively happens. This 'scandal' of particularity becomes a scandal of particularism only for one whose notion of experience disallows the testimony and witness of others as contributing to one's own experience. Yet such a person, to paraphrase Aristotle's analogous statement, is not a human being but either a god or a beast. For human beings to recognize the ethical call of the authentic interest of autonomous, critical reason is not to disallow disclosive and transformative testimony from others. Above all, it is not to disallow the testimony of an historical event—a life—which witnesses that the deepest possibility for human beings is in fact the impossible possibility of a life of authentically agapic love proclaimed and manifested as present now through God's self-disclosure in Jesus the Christ.

The category of the classic, therefore, should be extended beyond texts to those events and persons referred to (in front of, not behind) the text. The notion of experience outlined in Part I not only allows but encourages the testimony of those particularly intensified experiences of events and persons whose classical status assures their at once universal and properly revelatory status. It was not mere happenstance that William James, who helped to formulate the revised notion of experience, also sought in his *Varieties of Religious Experience* to search out the meaning of those most intense forms of religious experience, the mystic and the saint, as testimonies, in his language, to the 'strenuous life' par excellence.

For anyone who has actually experienced the transformative possibility for human existence disclosed in Jesus the Christ, either more immediately through proclamation and manifestation, or more mediately through interpretation and critical reflection, that event has all the force of a decisive revelation of both God, one's self, and, indeed, the final meaning of the whole of reality. For those whose notion of experience is in fact empiricist that event is likely to be expressed in a fundamentalist form—whether theistic or atheistic. For those whose notion of theological discourse discourages reflection upon the relationship between first-order religious discourse and second-order conceptual and reflective theological discourse, that event is likely to lead either to the Kierkegaardian comic dilemma of the Hegelian philosopher or the defensive *pathos* of the neo-scholastic conceptualist. For those whose notion of autonomy disallows the testimony of the authentic witness, martyr, saint, that event is likely to attempt a divorce between the event and person of God's revelation in Jesus Christ and the existential meanings of the texts expressing that event. For those, however, whose notion of experience is sufficiently wide to encourage an exploration of intense, old and new, religious experiences, and whose notion of hermeneutics is sufficiently sensitive to the intrinsic relationship between intense personal experience and its genre-expression in classical texts, events, and persons, then the seemingly tired and merely conceptual category 'revelation' becomes authentically experiential. Then the decisiveness and universality of God's revelation in Christ Jesus is recognized as both particular and universal, neither particularist nor universalist. When those same persons allow the corrective truth of the socio-critical power of Christian revelation play its central rôle, the temptation of hermeneutical theologies to retreat into a mere traditionalism will be disallowed and the temptation of empirical theologies to become merely individualist or weakly personalist in the manner of 'the New Narcissism' will be disowned. The experience of revelation is always itself revelatory; the revelation of God in Christ Jesus is radically experiential; when it occurs it cannot but be decisive in its transformation of both self and world by the God thereby disclosed; it cannot but be universal and definitive. In the meantime, we are presently witnessing in theology the many paths of a strenuous pluralism. Along those paths we all struggle—through theories of experience, of genre, of hermeneutics, of tradition and critique—to find the reflective discourse equal to that same liberating meaning, that same disclosive and transformative possibility first expressed in the parables of Jesus and in the confessions of the New Testament community that Jesus Christ is Lord.

## Bibliographical notes

For work referred to in this article, see:

Gadamer, Hans-Georg, *Wahrheit und Methode* (Tübinger, 1965)

Ricoeur, Paul, *Interpretation Theory* (Fort Worth, Texas, 1976)

Ricoeur, Paul, 'Hermeneutic of the Idea of Revelation', in *Harvard Theological Review*, vol. 70; 1-2 (Jan.-April, 1977)

Meland, Bernard E. (ed.), *The Future of Empirical Theology* (Chicago, 1968)

For more extensive development and citation of the new resources, the reader may refer to my forthcoming book (1979) *The Analogical Imagination in Systematic Theology* (Seabury) where the notions of 'classic' texts, events, persons and revelation are developed at length.

Heinrich Stirnimann

# Language, Experience and Revelation

## INSTEAD OF A TEXT

GOTTFRIED Keller, a writer who was nurtured on the spirit of liberalism, and well-acquainted with Feuerbach, wrote about his early youth in his autobiographical novel: 'However much I respected the good God and considered him in all cases, my imagination and heart were empty so long as I had no nourishment other than existing experience'. Keller had already referred to the Bible stories which his mother, widowed early in marriage, told her only son in a pious yet sensibly enlightened spirit. The text I have cited refers to an important Christian potentiality of experience: one based on the biblical narrative. Not only is the sense of the story fed by experience, but experience itself is intended to lead to *new* experiences. And Keller declares: '. . . and if I had no spur to make any occasional prayer, well God was a rather colourless and boring person for me, who asked me to do all kinds of musing and odd things . . .' Here he refers to a further possibility of experience: prayer on the basis of biblical proclamation (for Keller the Our Father is a paradigm of Christian prayer). Narrative and prayer are basic linguistic forms which enable experience in faith to be accommodated and passed on, retained and explained.

## THE PROBLEM

Problems are various. An acute awareness of problems can vary and usually recurs after a few years. The attempt to work out a nagging question can last for years. The variations of theology in the last few decades are well known. A few key words will recall the most important stages. As a result of the 'demythologization' debate, the hermeneutical debate itself reached a virulent stage. This confrontation was dissolved by the project of 'orthopraxis' which came into being

117

under the pressure of political events, and was presented as a critique of the supposedly sterile hermeneuticists. Yet the protagonists of 'political theology' soon gave way to the more fashionable 'charismatics' and 'pneumatics'. The 'theology of experience' and 'experiential theology' seem especially popular at present.[1] Ebeling's essay on the 'deficit of experience in theology' is not only significant for that reason, because a prominent theologian says what he thinks of a contemporary problem, but because the plaint about the lack of experience in theology is appropriately formulated.[2] Even though in his 'encyclopaedic tendency,' the author of *Wort und Glaube* denounced the threatened unity of theology in present-day research. In a study of the problem of experience, he rejects unsuitable solutions: 'the appeal to an optimally secure location in the everyday' and 'fanciful scientific abstraction'.[3] Empiricism has to be treated critically before integrating it into theology. It cannot be a matter of filling the experience gap in theology at the essential point—experience in faith—by the mere insertion of empirical content. Finally, Ebeling refers to the fact that both 'experience' and 'practice' come very close to hermeneutics, and are even partial aspects of that very question.[4] The gulf between past and present experience is constitutive of the hermeneutical situation, and difficulties in understanding cannot be answered by theory pure and simple but only by transformed practice. The dual terms 'faith-experience', 'faith-practice' and 'faith-understanding' which are significant in the history of theology, summarize the hermeneutical problem in theology as mediated through language. The well-known opposition of faith and reason on the other hand signifies an epistemological task in theology which is not reducible to hermeneutical reflection. It is more helpful than playing analytical approaches off against hermeneutical approaches to offer a scientifically theoretical definition of the presuppositions of understanding and to separate them from epistemological questions.

## THE ECUMENICAL RELEVANCE OF THE PROBLEM OF EXPERIENCE

The loss of the ecclesial community of faith was never a matter of 'pure doctrine' alone. The tragic event of the separation of the Churches is a matter of history, in which a number of cultural and political factors are concerned, and it is understandable only against a background of contradictory experiential claims. Separated Churches have developed different experiential traditions, whether sociological, psychological or spiritual. The restoration of Christian unity will become a reality neither by the addition nor by the subtraction of dogmatic or institutional elements, but only by reciprocal enrichment and greater profundity of faith, and by encounter and exchange of authentic experiences of faith in the community of the Holy Spirit.

I offer two examples drawn from the complex of theological problems. Attempts have been made at a phenomenological description of the main characteristics of the lives of the different Churches. In order to understand the Reformed understanding of salvation, emphasis was laid on the mnemic aspect of the recall of a past salvific action, and of the structure of hope, *non re, sed spe*. On the other hand, the insistence on the *present* aspect, the reality of salvation here and now, was shown to be typical of the Catholic understanding of salvation. More important than the discussion of the 'habitus' doctrine, and other speculative subtleties, is the metaphor *gratia infusa,* which is grounded in the language of the Bible. In view of the Protestant tendency to 'actualism' in the doctrine of grace and faith, and the associated practical over-emphasis on consciousness, the Catholic notion by which grace and faith are primarily to be understood as 'behaviour towards', and only secondarily as acts, is of more than mere doctrinal significance. An 'infused grace' without any essential reference to the 'living word' leads to the periphery of mythology and compromises what is specifically Christian.

Another example: the attitude to mysticism (which indirectly touches on questions of devotion to the saints). The Protestant reservations in respect to mysticism have to be studied carefully. Traditional objections concern the tendency to monism and pantheism inherent in mystical thought, the longing to obtain access to supernatural reality beyond mere faith, to connect 'directly', and the predominant influence of Neo-Platonism on the Christian mystics. Clarity is only possible here as a result of exact historical and comparative religious research. We should not forget the important connection between language and mystical experience, especially in Christian mysticism.[5] It is sufficient to mention the names of Symeon of the New Theologian, of Mechthold of Magdeburg and St John of the Cross, to evoke the creative power of mystical experience in a unique linguistic garb. The language of the mystics is to a great extent experientially— rich and contrasts strikingly with contemporary scholastic language. Finally, most mystical images, metaphors, similes, and so on, are echoes of faith-proven experiences of encounter with Scripture. Perhaps even the presently powerful wave of the charismatic movement—which is not to be confused with mysticism—will encourage ecumenical dialogue about the significance and originality of Christian mystics.[6]

Here I shall make only a few references to aspects of an enormous field of reference.[7] I have selected three aspects: (*a*) Experience that precedes the articulated language of faith; (b) experience in contact *with* the language of faith; and (c) experience opened up and made possible *by* the language of faith.

### EXPERIENCE AS A PRESUPPOSITION OF THE LANGUAGE OF FAITH

The fundamental condition for religious language is religious experience. This, according to Ramsey, consists of discernment and commitment. Commitment without discernment is blind bigotry, whereas discernment without commitment is hypocrisy.[8] Religious discourse suffers as much from a lack of discernment as from a lack of commitment. The fundamental objection against talk about God is based on 'a-religiosity': a radical inability of modern men to undergo religious experience. There is no point here in referring to the much and widely discussed problem of 'religion' except for a few remarks in relation to the theme of experience.

The continuous domination and manipulation of nature which many authors refer to in this context hardly constitute a diriment argument against the possibility of religious experience today. First, the destruction of nature can also lead to religious experience. Second, it is hardly possible to assert that the primary impulse of religious experience in archaic societies was a pure experience of nature. As far as we can discover, under those presuppositions too, it was primarily a question of confrontation with human fate. Furthermore, the 'atheism' of science, technology and of the structures of modern industrial society which is often mentioned in discussions of 'secularization' does not unconditionally argue against the possibility of religious experience in this context. Even if most traditional forms and models of religious expressions of life were to disappear, that would not mean the end of religion altogether. At present, we are experiencing a 'return to religion' that would have been thought impossible only a few years ago. It is not a question of peripheral phenomena and aberrant forms (for instance, exorcisms and fanaticism) but of a genuine longing for new and appropriate 'inwardness'. I should like to refer to another phenomenon which is not primarily religious in character: the attempt to offer new possibilities of experience in spite of the predominance of programming. In this respect we often encounter experiences whose openness to the religious dimension is hardly debatable. Symptomatic examples are the films *Spitzenklöpplerin* by Claude Goretta and *Kaspar Hauser* by Werner Herzog, which belong to the trend known as 'lyrical psychologism'. Both are expressed entirely in secular language, but so that, peripherally, authentic religious questions, those which concern man and the whole of his existence, can break out. Surely these and similar experiences in our present-day world enable us to speak of an intact religious language marked by discernment and commitment?

After these preliminary remarks on 'religious experience' I shall pose the question of the experiential basis of the Christian language of faith.[9] I start from the distinction in linguistics between active and passive linguistic competence. The passive linguistic competence is more inclusive and basic than the active. More important than a capability for 'talking' is that for 'listening'. But how is it that some hear the message of faith and yet do not listen to it, and others hear the same message and, affected by the proclamation, begin to speak? According to G. von Rad, in the perspective of the Old Testament the specific ground of understanding for the word of faith is 'fear of the Lord.[10] This indicates an experience of the *tremendum* and *fascinosum*. In fact, discourse in faith is hardly possible without this kind of fundamental experience of wonder and concern. Yet, especially from the viewpoint of the New Testament, it is not a question of 'dark' or 'hollow' or 'dim' experience. The experience which disposes to listening to the Christian message is that of being overcome by the story of Jesus. The *tremendum* and *fascinans* is the historic death of Jesus on the cross. 'Truly this was the Son of God!' [11]

But how do we pass from this condition of being affected to active Christian capacity for discourse? Neither the 'empty grace' nor the reports of 'appearances' are apt grounds for Christian proclamation. Only an experience of the Spirit allowed the breakthrough: the certainty that the Son of man 'had to' die and rise again 'according to the Scriptures'. That he truly rose again was something to which only that community was allowed to testify which experienced in the Spirit the living presence of its 'Lord'. The experience which loosens the tongue to speak of Jesus in assurance and joyous trust (*parresia*), is the experience of the Spirit in the community of the Church. 'Faith is not merely a cry'.[12] But a paradoxical experience is also possible in this regard. For nothing can make the credibility of the proclamation of Jesus so questionable as a Church that contradicts that message. Riches, prestige, ambition, self-assertion and calcified tradition destroy any real chance of experiencing a community assembled in Jesus. The paradox lies in the fact that only through the testimony of the Church does the story of Jesus become proclamation that pronounces certainty, and that nothing so hinders proclamation of Jesus as a Church which 'in practice' contradicts that message. Yet, in spite of many historical mutations, encounter with Jesus and participation in his community-founding and renewing Spirit remain the decisive experience which both entitles and forces one to engage in discourse in Christian faith. 'Woe to me if I do not preach the Gospel!'[13]

## EXPERIENCE OF THE LANGUAGE OF FAITH

I have tried to show that there is a form of experience preceding faith which enables one to hear the message of faith, and that there is also a form of experience which enables one to speak the language of faith. If one goes on to speak of experience *with* the language of faith, one means those experiences which the person who has arrived at faith experiences in faithful intercourse with the language of faith. From this viewpoint the state of being referred to the language of faith deserves to be mentioned first. Just as faith comes from 'listening'[14], so faith depends on hearing. Faith without the word of faith would be pure enthusiasm.

Ebeling distinguishes between three functions of the word: (*a*) 'making what is past present', (*b*) 'making the future present', and (*c*) 'disclosing what is hidden'.[15] I shall treat the first two functions together. We understand as the 'past' those events which are comprised in what von Rad calls 'canonical salvation history':[16] that is, the exemplary behaviour of God towards Israel up to the making visible of the Church through the sending of the Spirit. The 'Christ-event' occupies a central position here: the salvation 'fulfilled' in the death and resurrection of Jesus. This happening and this event are present in the word—and only in the word—of faith. We understand as the 'future' the coming of the Lord and the ultimate realization of the rule of God: the 'completion' of the salvation laid down and fulfilled in Jesus. This future is already effectively present in the word of faith. The terms 'past' and 'future' therefore refer to the two main aspects of the process of revelation according to the Christian understanding of faith.

I have not mentioned 'revelation' explicitly but only 'experience' and the 'language of faith'. Behind this reticence is a certain understanding of revelation that I cannot explain theoretically within the space of this article,[17] but shall only sketch summarily. As 'revelation' I understand neither an 'objectifiable' reality precedent to faith, nor a self-postulating and grounding 'transcendent' process. I understand as 'revelation' an event which presupposes the capacity of language and produces language. Only in and through the language of faith does the revelation-event become historically experiential reality. The basic determinations of this process are *language* and *word*. Only on this basis can we raise the question of 'existence in faith'. Since experience in relation to the process of the word is of a unique kind (it is neither to be produced, nor to be possessed, nor to be grasped), I used the term 'revelation'.

Hence the central event of experience of the language of faith is that in and through the language of faith the believer encounters the God who reveals himself to the believer: Jesus who has come to 'fulfil' God's salvific will, and Jesus who has come to 'complete' or 'realize' God's plan of salvation.

But encounter with the *viva vox Evangelii* is not the only aspect of encounter with the language of faith. There are also diverse experiences of the different expressions of historical tradition of faith. Only by means of traditional linguistic elements is it possible (at least in part) to conceive, objectify and test the process of tradition. In the objectivations of the process of tradition, both hermeneutical reflection and epistemological reflection enter in. It would be inappropriate—although this often happens—to use hermeneutical concerns as an attempt at total integration of a hypostasized tradition (and an equally hypostasized language) and to refer the task of criticism only to analysis. The hermeneutical consideration of chronological difference and human self-understanding pursues an eminently critical goal: revelation of the historical delimitation both of linguistic and of experiential possibilities in their whole extent. In the historical tradition of faith, there are various utterances and various experiences. Theologies come and go. Even dogmatic formulas change. Here we have the broad territory of critical church and dogmatic history. Yet we experience too the fact that Scripture, in spite of increasing chronological differences—is the source of renewal in the history of theology and in the life of the Church. That raises the question of the normative nature of Scripture.

Scripture was given to the community of faith as a 'memorial' (from which the effect of *pneuma* derives): 'These are written that you may believe'.[18] The central pronouncements, such as 'Jesus, Lord!'[19], 'Jesus, Son of God!'[20] and 'Jesus—yesterday and today!'[21] have a profound structure which is able still to work in a language of faith that is constantly changing in accordance with culture, age and individual experience. The biblical examples are especially significant for relation to experience: not only 'teaching' and 'confession' (the categories preferred by dogmatic theologians) but 'exhortation', 'consolation', 'comfort' and so on. The beginning and end of biblical paradigms are 'narrative' or 'telling', and 'prayer'. 'Narrative'—in accordance with biblical example, telling how God goes in search of man—is intended to bring men to look for God. Existence in faith is 'being on the way', and only someone who is 'on the way' is open to new experiences and ready for them.[22] 'Prayer' (that is, primarily according to the biblical pattern: 'petition') is a condition for staying on the way of faith. 'I believe, Lord help thou mine unbelief!'[23] That is probably sufficient to show how Scripture has a normative, indicative and paradigmatic character as a source of renewal in faith for proper intercourse with the language of faith.

## EXPERIENCE THROUGH THE LANGUAGE OF FAITH

In the foregoing I spoke of experience in faithful encounter *with* the language of faith. I speak now of experience *through* the language of faith, and refer by that to experiences which extend from the central point of Christian experience, encounter with the 'living word', to the natural dimensions of existence.

Experience is never a purely passive reception or suffering of something. The evidence of the empirical sciences is controlled. The data processing of a computer is programmed. Even the possibility of experiencing in other fields which obey less formal rules always depends on decisions taken beforehand. The thing that connects exact empirical information itself with spontaneous experience is language. Language conditions the structure of experience. A circle, or—more exactly—a spiral, cannot be avoided here too.

What experiences are especially relevant when speaking of experience *through* the language of faith? People are inclined to posit a scale of values and to say that historical experience, for example, is more important than experience in mathematics; or that psychology and sociology have more to do with the world of faith than, for instance, physics. Yet Ramsey has indicated that there are not insignificant analogies between mathematical and religious experience.[24] Ebeling and Jüngel have spoken, in regard to the reference of Christian faith to experience, of 'experience *with* experience', and even of 'divinely appropriate experience with *all* experience'.[25] In view of the universality of the rule of God and of the catholicity of Christian faith there is no area of human experience which can be excluded from contact with experience through the language of faith.[26] It would be particularly disastrous to assert that 'inward experience' in a subjectivist sense, or 'religious experience' in a pietistic sense, were especially privileged models of experience for experience through the language of faith.

## THE NATURAL MAN

The decisive question of the problem under discussion is: what is the meaning of experience through the language of faith as far as the natural dimensions of existence are concerned? This must not be taken too optimistically or too pessimistically. If one emphasized the basic openness of experience through the language of faith to all areas of human experience, then one would have to refer to the necessary concentration, the core and origin of all experience. The railhead, as it were, from Christian experience in faith to experience of the world is the experience of the experience of life. What the believer experiences first of all, on the basis of the *metanoia* of faith, is an opening up to the possibility of a new existence: existence in the 'freedom of the children of God'. At the same time, however, the believer experiences the continuing power of the law: his actual retention in the condition of the 'old man', which stands against the conversion to a 'new creation'. That which persists through the changes of the stages on the road of life is neither continual growth nor progress upward nor a peaceful existence. What is experienced as the fruits of testing (through the language of faith) is a more profound, really lived knowledge of 'what is in man'. This 'what is in man' comprises the entire natural constitution of man: his radical closure *and* the possibility of entering into active communication; his almost total fragmentation *and* his longing for wholeness; his thousand contradictions *and* his fundamental reliance on truth and integrity. What is to be experienced through the language of faith is not only the mere presence of the antinomies that permeate existence (which is alien to no genuine experience of life) but much more the *radical nature* and the *identification* of the antinomies which go to make up man. What happens in experiences through the language of faith may be expressed in the inclusive term 'disclosing what is hidden'.[27] What is 'disclosed'—through the word of faith—is the natural self, the contradiction and the possibility of a new existence in the world which is only possible from God.

## SCIENCE

Yet the experience of life is not to be reduced to self-knowledge. Life-experience includes both social partnership and deep-rootedness in the terrestrial and even the cosmic environment. Whatever develops from this point extends also to all areas of human experience. As examples, I cite three dimensions of experience which are especially relevant for present-day experience of life. First there is the experience of the sciences, or experiences mediated through science. Scientific knowledge has become a determinative factor of the complex society. Theorists of sciences are convinced that for future development not only a theory of theory-formation is needed but, much more urgent and important, a pragmatics and an ethics of scientific research. But this raises problems to which experience gained through the discourse of faith has something to contribute. It would be disturbing, to say the least, if Christians merely complained unimaginatively and made no constructive counter-suggestions based on 'experiences with experiences'[28] when confronted with the fact that the general thrust of the sciences and the means required to advance them are almost entirely governed by considerations of profitability and scarcely disguised egotism.

CULTURE

Another dimension of experience is that of cultural achievements and products. By 'culture' I do not mean 'humanism' in the sense of the fifteenth and sixteenth centuries. 'Culture' has nothing to do with 'aestheticism'. And the true bearers of culture are not to be found in the upper social élite. 'Culture' is a many-sided and broadly-based phenomenon and comprises not only major achievements (such as Mars probes and intercontinental jets of the Concorde variety) but the 'sub-culture' and the 'anti-culture' and even things that are thought of as 'non-culture'). What is especially requisite in a time of cultural mutation and revolution is a vigorous and resonant form of cultural *criticism*. That raises vital questions which experiences won from faith-discourse can also say something about. In the midst of the collapse of almost all conventional notions of culture we are concerned with nothing less than the need to provide a new image of man. And who would say that the experience of Christians had nothing relevant to say in this regard about the future of mankind?

POLITICS

Finally, I would cite the experience of political reality as the most inclusive dimension of the experience of natural existence. Political reality includes of course political programmes, concepts and ideologies. The moving force in all this is longing, need and striving for an ordered communal life and simultaneous satisfaction of the claims of freedom and justice. The fact that experiences gained through faith-discourse can also offer something positive in this respect is unquestionable. Surely talk of 'justification' has something to do with social justice.[29] The biblical models are especially important in this connection. It is sufficient to refer to the categories of 'neighbour' (*plesion*) and 'stranger' (*ethnikos*), 'poor' (*ptochos*) and 'mighty' (*dynatos*), 'rejected' (*exo ballamenos*) and 'accepted' (*dektos*), to show the experiential potential of biblical discourse in regard to highly pressing problems and particularly in the present political situation. Of course we must be careful of a purely political interpretation of Scripture and of an uncritical and unreflective 'translation' of biblical statements into the jargon of political ideologies (for instance, the play on *resurrectio* and *insurrectio*). The kerygma of Jesus holds us duty-bound to identification with the rejected and the oppressed. What should emerge from 'suffering' shared experience with the rejected and the oppressed by virtue of the word of faith is not a new political 'utopia' but initially a realistic criticism of the existing repressive structures and systems, and then a *language of hope* which points to the future and when possible alters the degrading circumstances of the present.

Throughout the foregoing section of my article I have had to use a somewhat inelegant formula, 'experience through the language of faith'. This clumsy usage was intentional. We have to make a distinction between experience *with* the language of faith and experience *through* the language of faith for reasons of theological clarity and precision. For a faith-decision and an interpretation of natural existence are not one and the same thing. The effects of faith lead at first by way of the language of faith to the possibility of new experience. Only if these experiences are actually experienced can faith become effective as far as natural existence is concerned. What I hoped to show here was that the experiences that are possible in faith are of very great significance indeed. What we can experience through the language of faith both in personal and in social and political life can be indicated in the 'disclosure' of 'hidden' possibilities. If we enter upon such a course in a condition of openness to experience, then the salvation-event—in and through the word of faith—attains its due fulfilment on the way of faith. As far as the natural dimension of existence is concerned, this fulfilment 'on the way' may be characterized with the terms 'endowing with meaning', 'awakening hope' and 'building community'.

## AXIOLOGICAL REMARKS

After the foregoing considerations I have to show what the consequences are for theology and theological methodology. To do this adequately I would have to write another article. All I can do here is to make a few remarks that point in the right direction.

Recourse to an *empirico-critical method* in theology—as a complement to the historico-critical and dogmatico-systematic methods—must be undertaken with care. First one has to try to find out what 'empiricism' and 'empirical' might meaningfully signify in the context of theology. I have already tried to make a distinction between 'experience' proper and 'experience of revelation'. A more detailed examination is necessary of the extent to which a properly 'empirical methodology' is applicable on the basis of what I have described as 'experience' before, with and through the language of faith (quite apart from 'experience of revelation'). The possibility, indeed the utility and necessity, of research into the life of the Church with the means of empirical sociology of religion and psychology of religion are not in question here. The problem is much more one of whether our experiences of faith and experiences in faith can be studied with the means afforded by the empirical sciences and, if so, to what extent.

Of course there is no doubt about the fundamental connection of theology with experience. Theology is not a purely speculative or theoretical science. The constitutive meaning of history, and of the tradition of faith, means that initially we have to examine the connection of theology with experience as a relation to biblical experience. In this regard Harvey Cox has offered valuable insights.[30] Theology is not only required to say exhaustively what the Church should be, but must first think about the actual state of the Church. The fact that in this process 'popular religion' requires more attention than is usual among theologians is an important finding. The first rule must be: theology is only being pursued with a real relevance to the actual nature of faith, if it is rooted in faith as it is lived and experienced. This rule does not offend against the duty of theology to examine the process of tradition critically. In addition theology must research into the present-day possibilities of experience. In the course of that research it has to analyze both the content of kerygma and the structure and location of possible experience. The second rule is: theology is only pursued with a real relevance to the actual nature of faith if it is able to open up really possible roads to experiences in faith (and if it is not obfuscated by abstruse theorems). If this rule is not obeyed, then theology is irrelevant to the history of faith.

The most important question is that of the extent to which experience should be treated as a criterion of theology. It is undeniable that the authenticity of experience, and above all of the experience of faith, is a criterion, indeed *the* criterion of truth. It is a task of theology to offer information on and evaluations of the authenticity of experience on the basis of the language of faith—and especially the word of faith.

*Translated by John Maxwell*

*Notes*

1. An indication of this is the considerable reputation of Marcel Légaut's books. For the reaction of theologians to the changed situation, see Harvey Cox's works, and D. Sölle, *Die Hinreise* (Stuttgart, 1975).

2. G. Ebeling, 'Die Klage über das Erfahrungsdefizit in der Theologie als Frage nach ihrer Sache', in *Wort und Glaube* III (Tübingen, 1975), pp. 3-28.

3. G. Ebeling, *Studium der Theologie, Eine enzyklopädische Orientierung* (Tübingen, 1975).

4. Cf. my article 'Erwägungen zur Fundamentaltheologie', in *Freib. Zeitschr. f. Philos. u. Theol.*, 24 (1977), pp. 291-365, esp. pp. 348-50.

5. Cf. especially, A. M. Haas, 'Die Problematik von Sprache und Erfahrung in der deutschen Mystik', in W. Beierwaltes, H. U. von Balthasar & A. M. Haas, *Grundfragen der Mystik* (Einsiedln, 1974), and idem., 'Die Struktur der mystischen Erfahrung nach Mechthild von Magdeburg', in *Freib. Zeitschr. f. Philos. u. Theol.*, 22 (1975), pp. 1-34.

6. In his book *Fremdheit als Heimat* (Fribourg, 1974), R. Friedli has referred in an original way to the significance of the mystical category of 'alienness' as a criterion for dialogue between the religions.

7. Cf. J. P. Jossua, 'Christian Experience and Communication of Faith', in *Concilium*, 9 (1973); J. Wunderli, 'Gibt es eine persönliche Gotteserfahrung?' in *Stimmen der Zeit*, 194 (1976), pp. 824-30; G. Zasche, 'Bemerkungen zum Verhältnis von religiöser Erfahrung und religiöser Sprache', in *Zeitschrift für katholische Theologie*, 99 (1977), pp. 183-94.

8. I. T. Ramsey, *Religious Language* (London, 1967), p. 18; cf. 14-37.

9. In regard to this complex of questions which seems so demanding to 'theonomically' educated ears, I would refer to the fundamental relation of 'experience' and 'natural theology' as discussed by G. Ebeling, especially in *Gott und Wort* (Tübingen, 1966), W. Pannenberg *Wissenschaftstheorie und Theologie* (Frankfurt am Main, 1973), esp., pp. 303-7, and J.-B. Brantschen, *Zeit zu verstehen* (Fribourg, 1974), pp. 90-8.

10. G. von Rad, *Weisheit in Israel* (Neukirchen, 1970), pp. 75-101.

11. Mk 15: 39.

12. H. Duméry, *La Foi n'est pas un cri* (Paris, 1959).

13. 1 Cor. 9:16.

14. Rom 10:17.

15. G. Ebeling, *Einführung in die theologische Sprachlehre* (Tübingen, 1971), pp. 53-5.

16. G. von Rad, *Theologie des Alten Testaments* II (Munich, 1968), p. 237.

17. For the most significant modern Catholic contribution to an inclusive 'theory of revelation' see K. Rahner. A summary account of this thought is available in the article on revelation in *Sacramentum Mundi*.

18. Jn 20: 31.

19. Rom 10:9; 1 Cor 12:3; Phil 2:11.

20. Rom 1:4; 2 Cor 1:19; cf. Acts 9:20.

21. Hebr 13:8.

22. Ebeling, *Wort und Glaube*, pp. 3-28 in his reflections on 'Experience as a

theological theme', starts from two of the existential determinations which characterize Christian life: 'testimony' and 'pilgrimage'.

23. Mk 9: 24.

24. Ramsey, op. cit., p. 36; cf. pp. 45 and 48.

25. Ebeling, *Wort und Glaube*, pp. 22, 25 f.

26. W. Pannenberg says in *Wissenschaftstheorie* that the verification of the notion of God has to include all dimensions of accessible experience.

27. Rom 10:17.

28. Cf. for example, C. F. von Weizsäcker, *Wege in Gefahr. Eine Studie über Wirtschaft, Gesellschaft und Kriegsverhütung* (Munich, 1976).

29. Cf. D. Mieth, 'Rechtfertigung und Gerechtigkeit', in T. Feiner, G. Gaudard, D. Mieth et al., *La Justice-Gerechtigkeit* (Fribourg, 1977), (pp. 64-89).

30. See n. 1 above.

# Contributors

PETER EICHER studied philosophy in Fribourg University, Switzerland, and theology at Tübingen, Federal Germany. He is professor at the Paderborn Polytechnical University in Federal Germany. He has published on Karl Rahner and anthropology, belief and revelation.

JAN HULSHOF, S.M., studied philosophy and theology at Lievelde and Münster Universities. His doctoral thesis was on truth and history and the work of Alfred Loisy. Since 1977 he has been a member of the General Directorate of the Marianist Fathers in Rome.

MATTHEW LAMB teaches in Milwaukee. Among his publications are studies of the religion between theory and practice in contemporary theology, and *History, Method and Theology* (1977).

DIETMAR MIETH studied German language and literature, theology and philosophy at the universities of Freiburg in Breisgau, Munich and Würzburg. He is professor of moral theology and director of the Institute of Moral Theology of the University of Fribourg, Switzerland. He has published on active and contemplative life, moral theology, poetry, faith and morals, and moral problems.

CARLO MOLARI was ordained in 1952. He studied theology in Rome and is professor of dogmatic theology at the Propaganda Fide University in Rome. He has published on theology and canon law in Aquinas, the language of faith and other theological questions. He is a member of the dogma committee on *Concilium* and national secretary of the Italian Theological Association.

BERNARD PLONGERON was ordained in 1964. He is a professor at the Institut Catholique de Paris, and research director at the National Centre for Scientific Research and course director of the Centre for

Religious Historical Research in Paris. He has published on the religious historiography of the French Revolution, theology and politics in the Enlightenment, popular Christianity, and clerical life in the eighteenth century.

WERNER SCHNEIDERS studied philosophy, German language and literature and English language and literature in Münster University. Since 1963 he has been a research-worker in the Leibniz Research Centre of the University of Münster and has taught in the philosophy seminar at Münster. He has published on law, morality and love, Karl Jaspers, natural law and the ethic of love, and the German Enlightenment.

ROBERT SCHREITER, C.PP.S., is dean of the Catholic Theological Union in Chicago where he also teaches systematic theology. He has published a number of articles in the areas of Christology and hermeneutics.

HEINRICH STIRNIMANN, O.P., studied art, philosophy and architecture in Lucerne, Zürich and Fribourg, Switzerland. He became a Dominican in 1942. He taught at Tallaght, Dublin, and fundamental theology at Fribourg. Since 1964 he has been director of the Institute for Ecumenical Studies and since 1966 co-president of the Evangelical-Catholic Dialogue Commission in Switzerland. He has published on ecumenism and the papacy.

DAVID TRACY is a priest in Connecticut and professor of philosophical theology at the Divinity School of Chicago University. He has published *The Achievement of Bernard Lonergan* (1970) and *Blessed Rage for Order: New Pluralism in Theology* (1975). He is editor of the *Journal of Religion* and of the *Journal of the American Academy of Religion*.